BY THE EDITORS OF CONSUMER GUIDE®

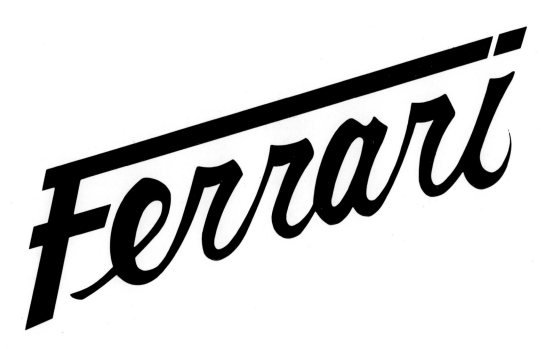

Ferrari

The Sports/Racing And Road Cars

BEEKMAN HOUSE
New York

CONTENTS

Louis Weber, President
Publications International, Ltd.
3841 West Oakton Street
Skokie, Illinois 60076

Manufactured in the United States of America
10 9 8 7 6 5 4 3 2 1

Library of Congress Catalog Card Number: 82-61173

ISBN: 0-517-381982

This edition published by:
Beekman House
Distributed by Crown Publishers, Inc.
One Park Avenue
New York, New York 10016

Credits

Principal Author
Godfrey Eaton

Photo Credits
Alfa Romeo U.K., Ltd.
William L. Bailey
Dean Batchelor
Godfrey Eaton
Ferrari Owner's Club of England
Geoffrey Goddard
David Gooley

Charles M. Jordan
Bill Kilborn
Modena Engineering, Ltd.
Joe Marchetti's International Autos
Ralph Poole
Graham Robson
Sports Car Club of America
Mel Weiner
Nicky Wright

Jacket Design
Frank E. Peiler

INTRODUCTION

Whenever automobile enthusiasts talk about racing, the name Ferrari inevitably enters the discussion. And if the conversation should turn into a heated debate over who builds the best engineered, the best performing, the most exciting and memorable road cars in the world, again the name Ferrari is sure to be heard.

Think about that for a moment. A number of marques can point to a long string of successes in international competition — grands prix, rallies, endurance events. Others can boast of commercial success as builders of passenger cars. Still others are known primarily for their technical innovations or trend-setting styling. But the number of marques recognized as leaders in all three of these areas can be counted on the fingers of one hand. Duesenberg comes to mind, as does Bugatti, though neither built cars in anything approaching significant numbers. Some would argue makes like Alfa Romeo, Maserati, Porsche, and Mercedes-Benz also qualify. But there can be no disputing Ferrari's position in this elite group. In fact, the combination of superlative performance, peerless styling, and uncompromising engineering excellence that characterizes virtually every Ferrari ever made is unique. Down through the years, this special character has imbued the cars that bear the prancing horse badge with the quality of being "remote," out of the ordinary — designed and reserved for a fortunate, privileged few. From this has emerged the mystique that surrounds Ferrari cars today.

The personality of Ferrari automobiles reflects the personality of Ferrari the man. Like so many of the great automotive pioneers, Enzo Ferrari grew up with the car, the automobile industry, and automobile racing. He was as fascinated with the glory and danger of competition as with mechanical detail and technical perfection. Much of this came from his father's influence. Later, he would work alongside the top engineers and race drivers of his day.

Very early in life, Enzo Ferrari dedicated himself to building the best race cars possible. He would later expand that ambition to include applying the lessons learned from racing to create what some have called the world's greatest road cars. He worked toward this dream through the difficult early years in his capacity as racing team manager for Alfa Romeo. There he proved himself to be not only a skillful driver but also a competent, creative administrator, with a gift for picking the right people for the right job and inspiring them to give their best. In the face of the Great Depression, Ferrari set out on his own to make racing pay, organizing Scuderia Ferrari as an independent team. It quickly became one of the most successful such ventures in European racing history. More importantly, it set the stage for the Ferrari road cars to come.

Ferrari racing cars have been seen in major events throughout the world in every year since 1947, a remarkable record. Though not all the racers were successful on the tracks, their influence on the design of Ferrari's contemporary passenger cars has been considerable. It's a tradition that continues to this day, and looms large in the Ferrari mystique.

So, too, does the power and performance of Ferrari engines. Enzo Ferrari believed the powerplant was the heart and soul of a car. He particularly admired the V-12 configuration, and no doubt carefully studied such engines built by the likes of Maserati, Hispano-Suiza, and Alfa Romeo in the 1930s. Thus, the very first cars to come from the new Ferrari factory in Maranello in the years immediately following World War II were V-12 powered. But Enzo was not blinded by the glamour of large multi-cylinder powerplants, and over the years he and his technicians demonstrated remarkable flexibility in designing both engines and cars to meet specific requirements. These included inline four-cylinder units, inline sixes, V-6s, V-8s, even horizontally opposed 12-cylinder engines. Again, not all these were successful, at least not immediately, but they would be ultimately through the sort of painstaking detail development that is also part of the Ferrari mystique.

Another element in the Ferrari legend is the dual-purpose character of many models, especially the early ones. The 166 Spyder Corsa or the 166 MM barchetta roadster were cars you could drive to the track, race, and then drive home again. In the 1950s, the idea of the race-and-ride sports car was extended through a succession of memorable models, each setting new standards of performance, versatility, even practicality. By the end of the decade, the concept had reached its peak in the 250 GT series of long- and short-wheelbase coupes, the competition berlinettas that, with only a few modifications, could be made into perfectly suitable, perfectly civilized street machines. In 1962, Ferrari introduced the superlative GTO, surely the most romantic, the most charismatic sports car of all time.

In Italy, form is never very far from function, and there's no better example than the many custom-body builders and designers who still flourish long after the heyday of custom coachwork in the '30s. Despite his emphasis on race-bred performance and engineering, Enzo Ferrari never forgot the importance of style and beauty in his cars. As a result, some of the most beautiful automobile bodies ever created have graced Ferrari chassis. Though *Il Commendatore* forged close relationships with all the major Italian design firms, it is the work of Pininfarina that stands out. This *carrozzeria* built more bodies for Ferrari than any other, and its design concepts were arguably the most innovative and aesthetically correct. Because of its small size, Ferrari has never built cars in great numbers, so it was logical and more economical to contract body work to an outside concern like Pininfarina. In the '50s, Ferrari built chassis with fairly standardized specifications only in very small numbers, so many bodies were crafted only one at a time and were one-of-a-kind designs. The very individual nature of the cars built in Ferrari's early years is yet another manifestation of the marque's mystique.

Ferrari's road cars would diverge from its racing machines in the 1960s. Beginning with the lithe and lovely 250 GT Berlinetta Lusso, Maranello's "customer" models became progressively more civilized and more expensive. But they never lost the aura of competition breeding or the performance that results from it. Meanwhile, the race cars were changing to meet new rules and regulations and to take advantage of advancing technology and new design principles. By 1970, the race cars and road cars had little in common except for one key intangible: Enzo Ferrari and his single-minded pursuit of excellence that was destined to make his cars famous the world over.

This book is primarily the story of how Ferrari road cars evolved through the years through their various models and series. But there's no escaping the role of competition experience in their design: the link is as strong as steel. That's why you'll also read about these cars' racing record as well as that of Ferraris designed solely for competition. Through it all stands Enzo Ferrari himself, a gifted, occasionally temperamental, always private man who has become without question a legend in his own time. He is a legend because of the cars he created and the way he created them. And that legend will live as long as there are automobile enthusiasts to remember the great names, the great deeds, and the great cars.

FERRARI

THE MAN

Enzo Ferrari was born in 1898, almost with the birth of the automobile itself. The horseless carriage was still a cantankerous novelty in the years Enzo was growing up in Modena, but his father had seen the potential of this new device. The elder Ferrari owned a car, and had added a garage workshop to his relatively prosperous metal business on the outskirts of Modena. This was the atmosphere in which young Enzo was raised. While his father would have preferred him to study automobile engineering at a technical college, Enzo decided that practical experience had advantages over book knowledge.

Enzo's interest in auto racing was forged very early. His father would take him to local races where he would watch the powerful and cumbersome cars of the day battling it out on the dusty rutted tracks. His imagination was fired by seeing the likes of Vincenzo Lancia and Felice Nazzaro, who even then were famous drivers in Italy. Small wonder that Enzo Ferrari made it his ambition to join an automobile company involved with racing when he reached manhood.

World War I intervened, and the young Ferrari was discharged from the Italian army in 1918 after a serious operation. Shortly before this, his colonel had given him a letter of introduction to Fiat, but the automaker turned

Young Enzo pilots the CMN circa 1919, one of his first races. Inset: Enzo placed 2nd in the 1920 Targa Florio with his Alfa.

him down for a job. It wasn't long afterwards that Ferrari joined a firm run by a man named Giovanni. This business rebuilt surplus Lancia light trucks and converted them into limousines with bodies made in Milan. On a trip to that city Ferrari ran across Ugo Sivocci, who also had ambitions to go motor racing. He persuaded Enzo to work for Costrusioni Meccaniche Nationale (CMN), which built cars from parts obtained from the Isotta-Fraschini factory. Some of these cars were intended for racing.

Enzo Ferrari got his first taste of competition at the Parma-Poggio di Berceto hillclimb, managing a respectable 4th place finish against some stiff opposition. Sivocci then entered two CMN cars, one for himself and one for Enzo, in the 10th Targa Florio in November 1919, run over four laps of the Medium Madonie circuit, a distance of 268.5 miles. Sivocci placed 7th. Ferrari failed to complete the course in the allotted time, delayed (as were other competitors) by a village political rally, always a hazard in the Sicilian hinterland in those days.

THE ALFA ROMEO ASSOCIATION

In 1920 Ferrari joined Alfa Romeo as a race driver. There he found himself in the exalted company of Antonio Ascari and Giuseppe Campari, both top-class competitors. Enzo quickly proved he was in their league by taking second place in the 11th Targa Florio that October, driving a 6.1-liter (372-cid) four-cylinder Alfa 40/60. Ugo Sivocci had joined the Milanese firm earlier in the year to add strength to the racing department, which had been set up by Ing. Nicola Romeo. Romeo

was determined that his company would make a name for itself in competition.

For the 12th and 13th running of the Targa the firm had an improved version of its 4.25-liter (259-cid) four-cylinder Model 20/30, also known as the Type ES Sport. Ferrari finished 5th and 16th, respectively, in the two events. He took part in one more of the Sicilian races, the 14th, when the firm fielded five cars developed from the new six-cylinder RL model. Three had a capacity of 3.0 liters (183 cid) while Sivocci and Ferrari drove 3.6-liter (219-cid) cars. Sivocci won, but Ferrari retired.

By 1923, Enzo Ferrari was firmly entrenched in the Alfa establishment. From this point until the birth of his son Dino in 1932, he would compete only when time and his not always good health permitted. Another reason he cut back his race driving was that he was now much more involved in planning and design of Alfa's passenger cars as well as its sports/racing cars. Part of his job was to manage the firm's racing program, which was of the utmost importance. In those days, a manufacturer's achievements in racing were even more essential to sales of its production cars than they would be in the post-World War II era. It was a job that naturally suited Enzo, and he never lost his flair for it. He was always able to select the right people for any particular project (a talent that would figure heavily in later years when he began forming the Ferrari company). Encouraged by Alfa racing manager Giorgio Rimini, Enzo put together the team of Ascari, Campari, and Sivocci, which gained many successes in Italian events.

In the years immediately after World War I, Alfa and other carmakers carried on with their prewar designs, as expected. However, a move away from the large-capacity slow-revving engines typical of the day was already underway even before WWI, a trend not lost on the more far-sighted designers and engineers, including Alfa's. At the 1912 French Grand Prix, a team of 3.0-liter Sunbeams matched against cars with much greater displacement, took 3rd, 4th, and 5th overall after a total of some 955 miles. This proved that small-capacity cars were capable of competing on equal terms against the old lumbering giants. By 1921, a new generation of grand prix cars had appeared, with Fiat leading the way.

For 1922, grand prix regulations stipulated a maximum engine displacement of 2.0 liters (122 cid), a minimum weight of 650 kgs (1433 lbs.) and, for some unfathomable reason, a restriction on the length of the tail. These rules produced sleek, low-slung machines that had not only aesthetic appeal but reasonable aerodynamics as well. With minor variations over the years, this basic design would be the norm for Formula 1 right up through the late 1950s. The most successful early example of the new breed was the extremely fast and reliable inline-six-cylinder Fiat designed by M. Bertarione. In fact, it was so successful that Fiat's entry for the Italian Grand Prix at Monza frightened off no less than 32 of the opposition. Louis Coatelen, a brilliant engineer with the Sunbeam company in France, enticed Bertarione to design and prepare its contender for the 1923 grand prix season. Fiat, however, was not short of resources, including one Vittorio Jano. He came up with a 2.0-liter straight eight, which would be fortified by the addition of a new device known as a supercharger.

In the meantime, Ferrari had set his sights on making Alfa Romeo the leader among grand prix car constructors. As a first step he persuaded a brilliant young technician, Luigi Bazzi, to leave Fiat and to join him and Giuseppe Merosi in designing Alfa's first Formula 1 automobile, designated the P1. (Bazzi would remain with Ferrari as a very close friend and associate for the rest of his working life.) The 2.0-liter inline six-cylinder engine used in the P1 was inspired by the invincible 1922 Fiat 804. But the P1 never raced. Although a team was entered for the 1923 Italian Grand Prix, Sivocci was fatally injured during practice and, as a mark of respect, Nicola Romeo withdrew his cars from the race.

Within a short time, Vittorio Jano got a call from Ferrari, who needed him badly to complete the Alfa Romeo design team. Jano was not at home, but his wife told Enzo that she thought her husband would turn down the offer. But after listening to Ferrari, Jano signed the following day, and even persuaded some of his colleagues to come along. Merosi was predictably upset by this move since Jano would oust him as chief designer. (Jano would remain at Alfa until the outbreak of World War II, when he joined Lancia. He would team up with Enzo again in 1955 when Ferrari acquired Lancia's D50 V-8 grand prix cars.)

Alfa Romeo was now in a strong position as a race car builder, boasting some of the world's best designers and engineers. But there was no room for complacency—or failure. Either would certainly have an adverse effect on passenger-car sales. In those long-ago days, the subtle art of advertising we know now was nonexistent. The "hard sell" was in the way a manufacturer's products performed in the heat of competition: to sell cars you first had to show you could win. It's interesting to wonder what might have happened to Fiat's fortunes had Luigi Bazzi and Jano not defected to Alfa. Fiat was now without three key people, and eventually got out of racing while Alfa went from strength to strength for many years. Who knows what might have been had Fiat not turned down a young Enzo Ferrari for a job in 1919?

Alfa's new P2 was to be ready in time for at least one outing during the 1924 campaign. While a lot of new thinking went into the car's design, it was only natural that Jano incorporated some ideas from his last creation, the supercharged Fiat 805 with its 2.0-liter straight eight. The P2 engine was technically similar to the Fiat's, and the two cars even looked somewhat alike. Even so, Luigi Fusi, a member of the Alfa design team in those days, said that Jano brought new and advanced techniques to the P2 project, and that this was a major factor in its success. To Fusi, Jano was an engineering genius.

Whether it was because of Ferrari's influence or Jano's genius and iron discipline, the P2 engine was on the bench and running by March 1924, only a few months after being first set down on the drawing board. In later years, Ferrari was known for being able to shift his thinking at short notice as necessity dictated, so there is every reason to believe that he pushed Jano to get the P2 ready as quickly as possible. Jano could also make snap decisions, and once he had a concept in mind he made sure his co-workers kept up with him.

A brief review of the P2's specifications is in order here to illustrate the engineering typical of early-'20s racing machines. The body was the usual two-seat, open-wheel type with a medium-length tail (some later cars for long-distance events had an abbreviated tail so a couple of spare tires could be carried without exceeding the length restriction). The frame had C-section steel side members tapered towards the rear. Wheelbase was 103.3 inches, front and rear track were 51 and 47 inches, respectively.

The P2 engine utilized a two-piece cylinder block made of welded sheetmetal. A light-alloy crankcase was used, and the cylinder head was integral with the block. With a bore and stroke of 61 x 85mm (2.40 x 3.35 inches) displacement was 1987cc (121.3 cid). On a 6:1 compression ratio output was 134 bhp at 5200 rpm with single Memini carburetor or 145 bhp at 5500 rpm with twin carbs. Twin overhead camshafts running in 10 roller bearings were driven from the rear of the engine. There were two overhead valves per cylinder, inclined at a 104-degree angle and operated via finger rockers. A two-piece crankshaft was counterbalanced with 10 main roller bearings in bronze cages. The supercharger was Alfa's own design, and blew air into the carburetor. Ignition was provided by a magneto sparking one 18mm plug per cylinder. The four-speed transmission was in unit with the engine, and the gearshift was placed centrally in the cockpit.

Suspension was by semi-elliptic springs and friction-type shock absorbers front and rear. Mechanical drum brakes, both hand and foot, operated on all four wheels.

The first of six P2s built was ready for testing in early June 1924, and both Campari and Ascari drove it on the Monza circuit. Ascari also drove it in its debut race at Cremona later that month, and won easily at 98.31 mph over a distance of 200 miles. It was timed during the race over the 10-kilometer (6.2-mile) straight in excess of 121 mph. Bazzi, who had much to do with the P2 design, rode as mechanic on this occasion (cars were much less reliable in the '20s than they are now, so mechanics customarily rode along in races). Next, the P2 appeared at the Pescara circuit in July. Campari should have won, but he blew a tire and couldn't finish for lack of a spare. Interestingly, he hid himself and the car on a side road until the race was over so other drivers wouldn't know he had retired. Ferrari saved the day for Alfa by taking his RL model past the checkered flag first, ahead of a Mercedes.

The P2 had yet to be fully tested, so in August a team of four cars was entered for the French Grand Prix, which was also the European Grand Prix for 1924 (in those days one regularly scheduled F1 event was so designated). The nominated drivers were Ascari, Campari, Louis Wagner, and Ferrari, but Enzo sat out the race due to ill health. The opposition was strong, with French teams representing Sunbeam, Delage, and Bugatti, plus Fiat, Schmid, and a single American-made Miller to be driven by an amateur, Count Lou Zborowski. Up to that time, the 1914 French Grand Prix had been termed the most thrilling automobile race in history, but it would be surpassed for excitement by the 1924 event.

Page opposite: Enzo Ferrari storms by an enthusiastic onlooker in the Circuit of Mugello race in 1928. This page, left: Antonio Ascari behind the wheel of the Alfa P2. Below: The highly successful supercharged Alfa Romeo P2 in its 1926 form.

There were five race leaders: Henry Segrave and Lee Guinness (Sunbeam), Pietro Bordino (Fiat), Ascari and Campari (Alfa Romeo). After some 500 miles over the 14-mile triangular course, the burly Campari crossed the line to finish in 7 hrs. 5 mins. 35 sec. at an average of 71 mph, with Albert Divo in a Delage only 65 seconds behind. Ascari led for 14 laps, but was forced out three laps from the finish due to water loss.

Alfa Romeo had arrived on the racing scene. And they did it with style. Drivers and riding mechanics were dressed in brown overalls with the Alfa Romeo name emblazoned in white on the front. The cars were painted dark red and bore the firm's green *quadrifoglio* (four-leaf clover) emblem on a white triangle on each side of the hood.

Four P2s were entered in the Italian Grand Prix at Monza in September. For this event, the cars were fitted with two Memini carburetors. This, of course, increased fuel consumption, so the oil tank was relocated from the firewall to under the mechanic's seat and a 5.5-gallon reserve fuel tank was substituted. Sunbeam, Delage, and Bugatti did not send teams, preferring to wait for the Spanish Grand Prix later that month. However, Fiats, Schmids, and Chiribiris were in force. And for the first time since the war, Mercedes fielded a team, four straight-eight supercharged cars designed by Dr. Ferdinand Porsche. Fiat and Mercedes withdrew, so the event was postponed until October, but the field was still thin. Alfa won a somewhat hollow victory as Ascari crossed the finish line at an average 98.76 mph over 497 miles. Incidentally, this was the last race where mechanics were required to ride along, although racing authorities insisted that body width should remain the same on future GP cars, a rather curious anomaly.

Grand prix racing declined in 1925 due to three factors: the rising costs of running a team, the dominance of the Alfa P2s, and the announced rules for 1926, which set maximum displacement at 1.5 instead of 2.0 liters. The European Grand Prix at Spa in June saw the P2s in a virtual walkover. The Delages were all DNFs for lack of a blow-off valve on their new superchargers. With no opposition, the Alfa drivers decided to take a five-minute

ISSY (Seine)

Giuseppe Campari at speed in the Alfa P2 on his way to a narrow victory at the 1924 French Grand Prix at Lyon. Note mechanic riding in left seat, a requirement in GP racing until the mid-'20s. The 1924 French Grand Prix is remembered as one of the most thrilling races in competition history.

Campari by 19 minutes. Meo Costantini in a 1.5-liter Bugatti was third, and Milton placed fourth. Tazio Nuvolari, destined to become one of the world's finest drivers, practiced in a P2, but crashed when his gearbox seized.

The P2s had many successes in *formula libre* races in 1926-30, but were barred from Grand Prix events after 1925 because of the new displacement rule. Some of these were sold to team drivers, who then raced them as independents, but the factory bought them back in 1930 to run once more after carrying out a number of major modifications.

The Alfa Romeo P2 was the epitome of race car design in the '20s, when speed meant little without strength and stamina. Those were the days when grand prix races ranged from near 500 to over 600 miles run on tracks that were primitive compared to today's much smoother and safer courses. Pit stops for fuel and tire changes were frequent. Fuel was simply poured in from large cans by means of funnels. And there was no easy method of raising the car for tire changes. Needless to say, the top pit crews had to be as well drilled and efficient as today's highly specialized teams—maybe more so. The Alfa Romeo association provided valuable experience for Enzo Ferrari as a team manager in the colorful world of European racing in the '20s. But it was only the beginning: it was time for the next step on the road to greatness for Ferrari the man.

SCUDERIA FERRARI

For reasons best known to himself, Enzo Ferrari decided to leave Alfa Romeo in 1929 and to go into business on his own. At the time, he was probably unsure about what his new enterprise would be or what form it would

break during the race for a quick snack, which didn't go over well with the Belgian home fans. Ascari won, followed only by Campari: there were no other finishers! July saw the French Grand Prix run over the new steeply banked Montlhery circuit. Because this was a high-speed track, Alfa replaced the stubby tails used at Spa with the original streamlined bodywork and cut three slots on both sides of the tail. Delage and Sunbeam also fielded teams. Ascari crashed and was killed. Although Campari was some four minutes in the lead at the time, the Alfa team was withdrawn in Ascari's honor.

The Italian Grand Prix in September would decide the winner of the new World Manufacturers Championship inaugurated for the 1925 season.

Three P2s were entered for Count Brilli-Peri, Campari, and American Pete de Paolo. A few Type 35 Bugattis with engines debored to 1.5 liters (91.5 cid) appeared as a prelude to the new 1926 formula and, surprisingly, two straight-eight Duesenbergs with centrifugal superchargers arrived to be driven by Peter Kreis and Tommy Milton. De Paolo had declined an invitation to race his Indianapolis 500-winning Duesenberg because he was unwilling to turn his beautiful slim car into a two-seater just to conform to European rules. That's when Alfa offered him a ride. Delage didn't show. The P2 tails were modified yet again. The streamlined design was shortened by some 6 inches but retained the three slots as at Montlhery. Brilli-Peri bested

The Prancing Horse

A certain amount of confusion surrounds the advent of Ferrari's prancing horse emblem. One story concerns the Baracca family of Modena. According to this account, Enzo Ferrari had won a race on the del Savio circuit in 1923, and in honor of his feat was given a piece of fabric from the fuselage of the Baracca son's Spad S13, in which he was shot down in World War I. The fabric showed a black prancing horse. It has been suggested this emblem was part of the Baracca family crest, but there is no evidence to support the idea. However, Francesco Baracca commanded Sqadriglia 91a, which used the prancing horse (cavallino rampante) as its insignia. Enzo apparently liked the design, and adopted it as his own. Since World War II, it has also been carried on the tails of F86E Sabre and Fiat-built F104 G Starfighter jets assigned to Aerobrigata 4a of the Italian Air Force.

Another story, told by the late Battista Pininfarina, is more believable. This account says that Ferrari's brother served with and died in the same squadron as Baracca and that, because of this, the Countess Baracca suggested to Enzo that he should use the prancing horse on his cars as a memorial.

The original horse and the one used today by Aerobrigata 4a is a fiery-looking steed standing on both hind legs with a drooping tail. Over the years, Enzo Ferrari must have given some thought to the implications of this, because the logo on all his cars from 1933 on shows the horse standing on one hind leg and with an uplifted or "rampant" tail.

---

have. Alfa Romeo had given him a car dealership covering the provinces of Emilia Romagna and Marche; the former included his home town of Modena. Ferrari's shop serviced and repaired various Alfa sports cars owned by the sporting young gentry of the region, some of whom were very excited about the idea of racing their machines. It was here that fate took Ferrari by the hand.

In September 1929, Baconin Borzacchini had broken the world 10-kilometer speed record on the straight at Cremona in his 16-cylinder Maserati. To celebrate, the Bologna Automobile Club held a dinner to which all the local big names were invited. Of course, Enzo Ferrari was there. He sat between Alfredo Caniato, a young textile merchant who was also a keen but inexperienced amateur racer, and Mario Tadini, a wealthy and much-respected clothier. Ferrari told these enthusiasts about his new business venture over dinner. His idea was to form a racing team composed mainly of amateurs. Caniato had recently purchased a 1.5 Alfa from Ferrari, and had finished a respectable 6th in a local race where Tadini had come in 3rd. Both men knew Enzo had been in the thick of racing during his Alfa Romeo days, and had a great deal of respect for him. Enzo explained that his new organization would be a co-operative financed by a number of enthusiasts and, perhaps, by some suppliers to the automobile industry. (The latter prediction proved true as Pirelli, Bosch, and Shell Italiana pledged sponsorship money.)

On December 1, 1929 in the office of Modena attorney Enzo Levi, the *Societa Anonima Scuderia Ferrari* was formed. Caniato and Tadini put up the necessary capital, with a number of other enthusiasts contributing smaller amounts. Ferrari now sought help from the Alfa Romeo board of directors. The Great Depression was increasing its stranglehold in Europe and, like so many companies, Alfa was faced with severe financial problems. Enzo suggested that Alfa could go racing at much lower cost by buying into Scuderia Ferrari, which would run Alfas as a semi-official factory team. Alfa agreed. Ferrari needed a top-name driver to get the best deals from race promoters, so he approached Giuseppe Campari, who agreed to race for the Scuderia whenever he could spare time from his factory commitments. This arrangement worked quite well to start, though Campari later bowed out.

The first race for Scuderia Ferrari as a purely amateur team was the Mille Miglia in April 1930, and a trio of Alfa 1750s was fielded. Tadini was teamed with Siena, Caniato with Sozzi, and Carraroli with Luigi Scarfiotti (father of the late Lodovico, who drove for Ferrari after World War II). All retired at various stages, while the Alfa factory cars took the first four places.

Apart from his ability to select the right people for the right job, Enzo Ferrari often seemed to have the knack for being in the right place at the right time. One such place was Milan where, along with a host of other VIPs, he welcomed Achille Varzi, who had won the 21st Targa Florio in May, breaking a string of Bugatti wins going back to 1925. Varzi had won with the P2 he had bought from Campari in 1928. Ferrari's entries in the race were 1750s driven by Nuvolari (who finished 5th) and Count Maggi (who retired). Whether it was the euphoria of Varzi's homecoming or Ferrari's persuasiveness, the Alfa Romeo board agreed to release a P2 to Scuderia Ferrari at Enzo's request.

This car had been raced in Argentina by Vittorio Rosa, and was reworked before being turned over to the Scuderia. The modifications consisted of enlarging the bore from 61 to 61.5mm (2.40 to 2.42 inches) thus increasing displacement to 2006cc (122.4 cid) and output to 175 bhp at 5500 rpm. Front and rear axles and brakes from the Alfa 6C 1750 Gran Sport were adopted.

Originally, the rear springs were inclined inwards, but Jano decided they should be mounted upright, outboard of the chassis and close to the wheels, to improve handling. The oil tank was relocated from the cowl to a spot under what had been the mechanic's seat, and the fuel tank was housed in the tail, which now had a deep groove to mount the spare tire. The cockpit was enlarged, but without increasing body width. The magneto drive was altered, and the supercharger now drew the air/fuel mixture from the carburetor instead of blowing through it. The slightly bull-nosed radiator was restyled, being inclined and squarish as on the Gran Sport. The modified P2 was now extremely fast, though somewhat difficult to handle.

Campari's departure from the Scuderia didn't worry Ferrari too much, because he had signed on Tazio Nuvolari to replace him. In his first drive for the team, in the newly acquired P2, Nuvolari not only won the Trieste-Opicina hillclimb but also broke the course record. It was the Scuderia's first win. But after a long career, the P2 was now being outclassed by both the Maseratis and the Type 51 Bugatti. Nevertheless, Team Ferrari participated in 24 events during the 1930 season, and scored nine 1sts, five 2nds, and five 3rds; Luigi Arcangeli also won four road races in a 1750.

When the 1930 season ended, Ferrari started what was to become a tradition with him by hosting a dinner for the team. In the '50s and '60s he would hold annual press conferences, which grew out of these annual team dinners, as a preview of his cars and plans for the coming year. Generally speaking, Ferrari was tolerant with the press, no doubt because, as a youth, he had

Above: The Scuderia Ferrari team poses for the cameras at the 1932 Masaryk GP in Czechoslovakia. From left to right: Nuvolari, Sforza, and Borzachini. Below: Nuvolari accepts congratulations from the fans after winning the 1932 Italian GP.

ambitions to be a journalist. However, this did not mean he necessarily gave straight answers. In his later years, his relationship with the Italian press was always a love/hate affair. In particular, the press could never understand why he so frequently used non-Italian drivers on his grand prix team. Perhaps for this reason, there would be an unseemly howl whenever Ferraris lost a race, which they did frequently. But when they won, there would be banner headlines and all was forgiven.

During 1931, Scuderia Ferrari continued as an amateur enterprise. Drivers were eligible for a percentage of the prize money plus start and bonus payments, but those who drove their own cars were expected to pay servicing and repair bills. At this stage, Alfa Romeo was taking an increasing interest in the team, and allowed Ferrari to run one of its new 2300 sports cars in the Mille Miglia and other important races — but with factory drivers at the wheel.

Mario Tadini, the first president of Scuderia Ferrari, was becoming disenchanted with the way in which the professional element was not only creeping in but actually being invited by Ferrari. Accordingly, he sold out to Alfredo Caniato and resigned. He was replaced by Count Carlo Trossi of the Banco Sella banking family. Enzo was indeed moving away from his original idea of an amateur team because he wanted to make racing pay, and there was no guarantee there would be enough enthusiastic — and

The Alfa Romeo Type B Monoposto, *the legendary P3, in its 1932 guise.*

wealthy — amateurs around to keep the Scuderia going. Even though he resigned as president, Tadini continued to drive for the Scuderia, and gained quite a reputation as a hillclimb specialist. At one time, the Scuderia's transporter was emblazoned with the name of his clothing firm.

The Alfa 2300 performed well in 1931. It wasn't as fast as the Type 51 Bugatti, but it was more reliable. Nuvolari drove one to win the 22nd Targa Florio in May over 363.2 miles. At the Italian Grand Prix a new GP version of the 2300 appeared, and proceeded to win the 10-hour event, with Nuvolari and Campari sharing the driving. They were followed by Minoia and Borzacchini in a similar car. Following this, the cars had the Monza name tagged on to their designation.

The Scuderia's new president, Count Trossi, started the 1932 season by finishing 2nd in the Mille Miglia with a 2300; his co-driver was the Marquis Antonio Brivio. The winner, also in a Scuderia 2300, was Borzacchini, who shared his car with Bignami. Although an amateur, Trossi was a superb driver, far superior to many of the professionals of his day. The year also saw the introduction of Jano's 2.6-liter P3 Formula 1 racer, which made its debut at the Italian Grand Prix in June. Like the P2, it won on its first outing.

The P3 is one of the most written-about cars ever made. Its engine was similar to the straight eight in the 2300 sports cars, with the same 65mm bore, though stroke was increased from 88 to 100mm (3.46 to 3.94 inches). The alloy cylinder head was non-detachable. Two small superchargers were used instead of the single large unit in the sports car, each working on a single Weber carburetor in Scuderia trim or a single Memini or Solex in factory guise. The transmission was novel, with the drive split from the differential (incorporated behind the gearbox) through two torque tubes running to the rear axle, forming a V. The axle itself was a light tube and the halfshafts short stubs. The gearbox was the weak link since it was the same one used on the sports cars and could withstand only 150 bhp versus the 215 bhp of the P3.

Before 1933, Scuderia Ferrari had not had full control of the Alfa racing program. It wasn't easy to tell the cars entered and raced by the Scuderia from official factory competitors. But at the end of 1932, Alfa decided to hand over all its racing activities to Scuderia Ferrari. The reason: Alfa Romeo was in very bad financial shape now, so much so that the firm came under government control. The racing

department was all but shut down. Rudi Caracciola, one of the finest drivers ever to come from Germany, had a contract with Alfa Romeo, and was advised to join Scuderia Ferrari for the 1933 season. Apparently, he didn't like the idea of having Enzo Ferrari as his boss, for he formed a partnership with former Bugatti driver Louis Chiron and called it Scuderia C.C. (Caracciola-Chiron). It is difficult to understand Cariacciola's attitude because Ferrari was known as a forgiving administrator, even if a driver should break his car.

Alfa Romeo's withdrawal from competition included keeping its new P3 under wraps, so Ferrari had to rely on the earlier P2 Monzas. However, these cars couldn't keep pace with either the Maseratis or Type 51 Bugattis, so their engines were bored out to 2.6 liters (158 cid) for more power and speed. Ferrari had formed a close association with Weber, the carburetor manufacturer, and all his cars would be fitted with Webers from here on and into the 1980s. One other important change for 1933 involved insignia. In the past, Alfa's factory racers had worn the *quadrifoglio*. Now that Scuderia Ferrari was in charge, this was replaced by a shield bearing a

black horse against a gold backround (gold is the official color for Modena). This emblem would be seen on all Ferrari cars from then on.

The Tunis Grand Prix was the first race for the bored-out Monzas. Nuvolari came home in 1st place, followed by Borzacchini. The all-important Mille Miglia saw Nuvolari again outstripping the opposition. At Monaco, after a close race, he lost to his arch-rival Varzi. However, Nuvolari went on to win at Bordine and in the Eifel run at the Nurburgring. Then he blotted his record at the Tripoli Grand Prix. That race was run as a lottery, and he, Varzi, and Borzacchini worked a payoff deal with ticket holders. Varzi won in a Type 51 Bugatti, with Nuvolari only a length behind.

Ferrari, always a disciplinarian, had not always seen eye-to-eye with the volatile Nuvolari. After two differential failures (in the Penya Rhin Grand Prix at Barcelona and the Grand Prix de la Marne), Nuvolari left the Scuderia, and signed a contract to drive a *monoposto* (single-seat) Maserati.

While the 2.6 Monza was not always reliable, it was certainly

The archetypical GP car of the '30s. The Alfa P3 in action.

more successful this season than either the Type 51 Bugatti or the 2.9 Maserati. But in August, the Alfa Romeo board realized that the Maserati was a real threat to the Monza and, with pressure from Pirelli, at last turned over the new P3 to Scuderia Ferrari.

Meantime, Enzo acquired the services of Louis Chiron, one of the best French drivers in history if not the best, to replace Nuvolari. But it was Luigi Fagioli who won two important end-of-season races for the Scuderia, the Coppa Acerbo and

the Italian Grand Prix. Then tragedy struck at the Monza circuit, when the Scuderia's 4.5-litre 'Duesenberg' hybrid driven by Count Trossi threw a rod at the South Curve, and spilled oil on the track. This indirectly caused an accident in which Campari and Borzacchini were killed.

Formule libre racing was now at an end. The new grand prix formula for 1934-37 stipulated a maximum dry weight of 750 kilos (around 1650 lbs) and a minimum cockpit width of 850mm (about 33.5 inches). Maserati had its 2.9-liter car and Bugatti had more recently produced its beautiful 2.8-liter Type 59, so Alfa Romeo decided that, to keep pace, it had to enlarge the 2.6-liter P3 engine. Bore was accordingly increased from 65 to 68mm (2.56 to 2.67 inches) which with the 100mm

Page opposite, above: The start of the 1934 French GP at Montlhery. Louis Chiron takes the lead in the Scuderia Ferrari P3 Number 12. Below: Varzi makes adjustments to his P3 in the 1934 Marne GP. That's Enzo standing on the wall to the immediate left. This page, below: Louis Chiron hurls the P3 around the course at the 1934 Dieppe GP. Note the prominent cavallino rampante shield, symbol of Scuderia Ferrari, on the hood directly aft of the radiator.

stroke yielded 2.9 liters. The P3's previous four-speed gearbox was replaced by a three-speed unit. Wheelbase, track, and weight of the original P3 were also increased, and the factory designated the new car the Type B Monoposto. The body was wider, again to meet the new regulations.

The 1934 season saw the arrival of teams from Mercedes and Auto Union of Germany. It would mean the decline of Scuderia Ferrari as a force in grand prix racing until Enzo set up as a constructor on his own after World War II. Nonetheless, the Scuderia won 11 of the 24 main grands prix. Most of these came early in the year. Towards the end of the season as they gained in reliability, the German cars outstripped the Italian ones. Maserati and Bugatti both had larger engines, and were also faster than Ferrari's Alfas.

The last Le Mans win for a 2.3-litre straight-eight supercharged Alfa Romeo came in 1934 after four successful years in the 24-hour event. A new Jano-designed 2.3-liter six-cylinder car replaced it, and finished 1-2-3 on its initial outing in the Targa Abruzzo at Pescara. The winning car, driven by Francesco Severi and Franco Cortese, had a fairly streamlined closed body designed by Touring of Milan.

Nuvolari returned to Scuderia Ferrari for the 1934 season. There was no apparent reason for his change of heart, unless he had heard that Enzo and his chief designer Luigi Bazzi were cooking up a couple of special cars that would be a real driver's challenge. By now, both Enzo and Bazzi were frustrated with Alfa Romeo, which couldn't provide the hardware to match the Germans with their heavy financial backing from the Third Reich. The Alfas were plainly no longer competitive.

The result was the first racing cars designed by Ferrari and his friend Bazzi, built within a mere four months. Called Bi-Motore, it made liberal use of Alfa Romeo parts, including engines, with factory permission. Two of these were built, identical apart from engine displacement. The one built for Nuvolari had two 3.2-liter (195.3-cid) straight eights with a combined capacity of 6330cc (386.2 cid) and output of 540 bhp. Louis Chiron's car had two 2.9-liter (176.9-cid) straight eights for 5810cc (354.5 cid) and 520 bhp. One engine sat ahead of the cockpit, the other behind it.

The multi-plate dual-disc dry clutch was in unit with a constant-mesh three-speed transmission driven off the front engine, with the differential aft of the gearbox. The final drive was split into two angled propeller shafts with two crown wheel and pinion units. Twin transverse members located the rear engine, to which were attached two strengthened oscillating parallel arms with housings for the conical couplings that transmitted power to the wheels. Each wheel was linked to its housing by a short halfshaft, and could therefore move in a fashion similar to a swing-axle suspension. Also at the rear were two semi-elliptic leaf springs attached to the independently sprung wheels. The rear engine drove forward via a shaft passing through the gear mainshaft, which was hollow, the clutch engaging an internal toothed drive on the front engine flywheel. Drive from the rear engine could be disengaged by a hand-controlled dog clutch on the shaft. To start the car you fired up the front engine, then engaged drive to the rear engine which cranked that. The Bi-Motores used the Type B chassis lengthened by some six inches.

These unusual and powerful machines debuted in May 1934 at the *formule libre* Tripoli Grand Prix. Mechanically, they proved extremely reliable, but the tires couldn't withstand their power and speed, especially under the baking sun. Nuvolari had to make 13 pit stops just for tire changes, but finished 4th. Chiron was 5th. Later in the month the Bi-Motores ran at the Avus Grand Prix, staged in two 100-kilometer heats and a final 200km race. Tires were again a problem, and were the undoing of Nuvolari, who finished 6th in heat one (only the first four finishers in each heat went into the final). Chiron finished 4th in his heat. In the final, Chiron was cautious, but it paid off with a 2nd place result.

There were no further *formule libre* races, so Ferrari decided to

attack some world speed records with the Bi-Motore. To reduce overall weight, the two side fuel tanks were replaced by a single small tank. An aluminum disc was fitted to each wheel for added streamlining. In June on the Firenze-Mare *autostrada,* Nuvolari set two new Class B international speed marks: the flying kilometer at 199.92 mph and the flying mile at 200.77 mph. Thus ended the short career of this spectacular twin-engine car.

The Type B Monopostos were further developed during 1934. Nuvolari's winning car at the Pau Grand Prix in February had reversed quarter-elliptic springs at the rear, similar to those on the Type 59 Bugatti, and hydraulic shock absorbers instead of the original friction type. In April, at the LaTurbie hillclimb, Rene Dreyfus' car sported more modifications, independent front suspension and hydraulic brakes. Dreyfus also drove at the Monaco Grand Prix, where he finished second to Fagioli's Mercedes. This car had the older front suspension and an engine bored out to 71mm (2.79 inches) for 3165cc (193 cid) and 265 bhp at 5400 rpm.

The 1935 season was a reasonably successful one for Scuderia Ferrari. Although the Alfas weren't expected to match either Mercedes or Auto Union in major grand prix races, they usually gave a good account of themselves. For example, in the Eifel race at the Nurburgring, Louis Chiron followed Caracciola's Mercedes and Rosemeyer's Auto Union in his 3.2-litre Type B. He was even congratulated for his fine drive by the German teams, a gesture that would be almost unhead of in today's high-stakes Formula 1. For the French Grand Prix, both Nuvolari and Chiron had cars with the "full treatment." Bore was increased to 78mm (3.07 inches) boosting displacement to 3.8 liters (231.9 cid) and power to the region of 330 bhp. Nuvolari took the lead, with Chiron right behind him. Unfortunately, both

cars retired with rear axle failures, but at least Nuvolari had the satisfaction of setting a lap record.

Perhaps the greatest satisfaction for Scuderia Ferrari came on the opposition's home ground, the Nurburgring, in the German Grand Prix. Nuvolari drove his Type B like a man possessed to take the checkered flag (much to the chagrin of the home teams) in a race often described as one of the most memorable of all time. Back home, the Italian Grand Prix was held as usual at Monza, and Nuvolari had a new Alfa Romeo designated the 8C-35. It had a bulbous, high tail, all-independent suspension, and the 3.8-liter engine. Nuvolari set out to harrass the Mercedes and Auto Unions. One of his pistons went out later, but not before he had again managed to break a lap record. Never one to give up, Nuvolari took over Rene Dreyfus's Monoposto and gave chase to Stuck's Auto Union. A valve cried "enough!," so he had to be content with 2nd after driving many laps on only seven cylinders. Although some harsh things have been said about Nuvolari over the years, it is to his credit that he gave the prize money to Dreyfus.

The regulations for the 1935 Mille Miglia were apparently lax, because race officials overlooked a new Alfa prepared for Carlo Pintacuda. It was a 2.9-liter (176.9-cid) Monoposto that had been converted into a two-seater, complete with cycle-type fenders, a ridiculous top, and electric lighting and starting. The unfortunate, and surely cramped, passenger was the Marquis Della Stufa. Surprisingly, Pintacuda scored an easy win, finishing 42 minutes ahead of the second-place car, a Monza Alfa. Two other important races fell to the marque during the season. The Marquis Antonio Brivio won the Targa Florio in a Type B, followed by Chiron in a similar car; and Cortese and Severi won the 24-hour Targa Abruzzo in a 6C

2300 with closed bodywork.

While Scuderia Ferrari was outclassed in all the major grands prix except the German event, they had the legs of the Maseratis and Bugattis in the less prestigious races, placing 1st in no less than 14. Nuvolari was the most successful driver, winning on seven occasions.

Ferrari signed Nuvolari, Brivio, Giuseppe Farina, Pintacuda, and Tadini to drive for the 1936 season. Chiron moved over to Mercedes, and Dreyfus was contracted to drive the French Talbots. Count Trossi, erstwhile President of the

Scuderia, resigned. Enzo took his place.

Four 8C-35 Alfas were entered for the Monaco Grand Prix, which had to be run in pouring rain. The unfortunate Tadini completed only one lap, trailing a pool of oil around the track that resulted in a six-car pileup at the chicane on lap 2, eliminating much of the opposition. Caracciola led for 10 laps in his Mercedes before Nuvolari passed him, only to fall back by lap 27 due to failing brakes and a rough engine. However, Nuvolari did manage to take 4th.

A new Alfa Romeo was fielded

Alfa Romeo's 1936 Type C competed with both eight- and 12-cylinder engines. The straight-eight version was the more successful in European grand prix races.

for the Tripoli Grand Prix. This was the 12C-36 with a 4.1-liter (250.2-cid) 12-cylinder engine. In most respects it was similar to the 8C-35, and still lagged behind the 4.7-liter Mercedes and the 6.0-liter Auto Unions in displacement. Horsepower ratings were 494 for the Mercedes and 520 for the Auto Union, with the new Alfa way down the scale with a modest 370. The 12C-36 did not perform as expected at both Tripoli and Carthage. At each event, an 8C-36 finished ahead of the newer car. However, it vindicated itself at the Penya Rhin Grand Prix on the twisting Monjuich Park circuit at Barcelona, where Nuvolari crossed the finish line three seconds ahead of Caracciola's Mercedes and set another lap record in the process.

During the *Eifelrennen* at the Nurburgring, Nuvolari was ahead of the German cars. Then a thick mist descended. Perhaps because he was more familiar with the course, Rosemeyer (Auto Union) took the lead, and won by over two minutes. But Nuvolari continued to press the German machines even though he was down on power and speed. In the Hungarian Grand Prix at Budapest he won driving an 8C-35 by 14 seconds over Rosemeyer. After this, there was no stopping the man from Mantua. After a wheel-to-wheel battle with Varzi's Auto Union, he won the Milan race by a nine-second margin.

Scuderia Ferrari was certainly having a good season, bolstered by the return of Dreyfus. Brivio (12C-36) placed 3rd in the German Grand Prix. At the Coppa Ciano at Leghorn, the team scored a sweeping 1-2-3 finish with Nuvolari (8C-35) leading Brivio (12C-36) and Dreyfus (8C-35) ahead of the highest placed Auto Union. The only other race that season where the Scuderia placed was Monza, as Nuvolari's 12C-36 finished second to Rosemeyer's Auto Union.

At the end of the season, the Scuderia sent three cars and drivers to the U.S. for the revived Vanderbilt Cup series. The original run for the Vanderbilt trophy had been staged on a variety of tracks in 1904-06 and 1908-16 (except 1913). George Vanderbilt, nephew of series founder William E. Vanderbilt Jr., was keen to show the American public what road racing European-style was all about. Money was no object. The trophy

was commissioned from Cartier, and total prize money was $60,000, a third of that for the victor alone. Instead of settling for a cinder or wood-and-brick oval track typical of the day, Vanderbilt built a brand-new circuit designed by Major George Robertson. It was four miles long, with 15 fast straights and 16 short corners that put a severe test on brakes and gearboxes. Minimum width on the straights was 60 feet, increasing to 125 feet at the bends. The track's outer rim was formed by a continuous hub-high steel barrier, though openings were left at the most severe turns as safety exits. Eddie Rickenbacker of the Roosevelt Raceway Corporation supervised construction. It involved a six-inch base of hard-packed sand, gravel, and clay treated with a binder of slow-curing oil. This was then sealed by a top layer of tar-oil.

Race regulations limited cars to a 366-cubic-inch displacement. Single or two-seat bodies were permitted, as was use of replacement drivers. There was no restriction on fuel type or quantity. One strange provision was a mandatory one-minute pit stop that had to be made between the 40th and 60th laps for technical inspection. The race would cover 75 laps or a distance of 330 miles.

Nuvolari and Count Brivio were assigned to drive 12C-36s for Scudaria Ferrari, with Farina piloting an 8C-35. Outwardly, the three cars were indistinguishable except that the 12-cylinder machines had two side exhaust pipes running under the body and the eight-cylinder car had a single exhaust. Ettore Bugatti sent two Type 59s for Jean-Pierre Wimille and three-time Indianapolis 500 winner Louis Meyer. The latter was eliminated in practice when he spun and ended up straddling a barrier. Other European cars entered were Maseratis handled by Goldie Gardner, E. K. Rayson, Philippe Etancelin and Australian Freddy MacEvoy and a trio of British E.R.A.'s for Earl

Howe, Pat Fairfield, and Major S. S. Cotton. Raymond Sommer backed up Scuderia Ferrari with his own 2.9 Monoposto. Prominent U.S. drivers included Mauri Rose, Rex Mays, Bill Cummings, Frankie Brisco, Tony Gulotta, and Wilbur Shaw.

The 1936 Vanderbilt race was held on October 12th, which turned out to be a perfect, warm fall day. Incidents were few, although Shaw and Farina tangled with the steel safety fence, and Nuvolari and Litz got close enough to rub hubs. Of the 45 starters, 30 crossed the finish line, with the European cars outclassing the two-speed-gearbox American machines. Nuvolari's 12C-36 took the checkered flag, followed some two minutes later by Wimille. Brivio placed 3rd despite suffering ignition troubles. The highest finish by an American was Rose in 6th, followed by

Cummings. Nuvolari's average was 65.99 mph, which certainly didn't impress Americans used to higher speeds on the brick and dirt tracks. In fact, a *New York Times* reporter wrote: "A great many spectators hastened out to the Roosevelt Raceway at 50 mph, ducking cops all the way, to see Nuvolari win at slightly better than 65." The report ended sourly: "It didn't add up."

The Vanderbilt Cup was staged again in 1937 on July 5th after being postponed two days due to heavy rain. Team Ferrari fielded a pair of 12C-36s for Nuvolari and Farina. The 8C-35 driven by Farina the previous year had been bought by Rex Mays, who entered it as an independent. Mays modified the car by fitting a centrifugal supercharger, and it paid off. In practice, he was faster than the Scuderia cars, which did not please team manager Marinoni, and Mays found

himself on the front row. Mercedes sent over cars for Rudi Caracciola and Dick Seaman. Auto Union had Rosemeyer in its lone contender. The circuit had been altered so that only seven of the 16 bends remained and the straights were lengthened, all in the interest of higher speeds.

The race began with a big bang at 12:15 as President Franklin Roosevelt pressed a button to set off an aerial "bomb." Caracciola and Roseymeyer were followed closely by Mays, with Seaman, Nuvolari, Billy Winn, and Ernst von Delius filling the next four places. By lap 16, Farina had his 12C-36 in 5th spot. Lap 22 saw the disappearance of Caracciola, and Nuvolari blew his engine trying to out-gun Seaman. Nuvolari took over Farina's car on lap 40 and started to step up the pace. He passed Delius, and was chasing Mays when his engine faltered. He promptly

handed the invalid back to Farina, who ultimately took 5th place. Rosemeyer won at an average speed of 82.56 mph. He was followed by Seaman, with Mays one lap behind in 3rd. Mays might have been a lot closer to Seaman had it not been for a poor pit stop for fuel and a tire change that took a lengthy 1 minute 18 seconds. For a second time, the American cars had been outclassed. Russ Snowberger was the highest finisher in a 4.2-liter Miller. Joel Thorne, a young American millionaire driving an Alfa 2.9B monoposto, placed 6th.

Ferrari gathered his usual broad lineup of drivers for the 1937 season. Nuvolari, Brivio, and Farina were the stars. In its customary fashion the Scuderia

Two of Scuderia Ferrari's four 8C-35 Alfas before the start of the 1936 Monaco GP. Nuvolari was the highest placed team driver, coming in 4th.

notched its first season win at the Mille Miglia, which fell to Pintacuda in a 6C 2.3; Farina took 2nd in a similar car.

The home races in Italy were a boon for the Scuderia as the German teams rarely took part in these "minor" events. The eight- and twelve-cylinder Alfas took the circuit of Turin, the Naples Circuit and the Superba Circuit at Genoa. Auto Union sent but a single entry to the Circuit of Milan for the bespectacled Rudolph Hasse, but his journey was in vain as Nuvolari not only won outright but beat Hasse by a lap. It would be the last time Nuvolari would be able to better the German cars. Overall, though, 1937 was not a good year for Team Ferrari. Although Pintacuda's 8C-35 beat Stuck's Auto Union in the Rio de Janeiro Grand Prix, the team's year-end scorecard showed a mere four wins, all in minor events, against six major victories for Mercedes and five for Auto Union.

Alfa Romeo announced during the year that it would return to racing in 1938. Regulations were rewritten for that season, setting maximum displacement at 3.0 liters supercharged or 4.5 liters unsupercharged. There would be three new cars running under the Alfa Corse banner. One was the Type 8C 308, a further development of Jano's straight eight engine with bore and stroke of 69 x 100mm (2.72 x 3.94 inches) giving a capacity of 2991cc (182.5 cid) and 295 bhp at 6000 rpm. A V-12 car designated 12C-312 was outwardly a smaller edition of the earlier 12C-37, and had 320 bhp at 6500 rpm. Finally, there was the type 16C-316, with two straight-eight blocks and twin superchargers placed between. None of these cars took the grand prix scene by storm.

Neither did the 430-bhp 12C-37, so Alfa dismissed its long-time designer, Vittorio Jano, even though little development work had been carried out on it. Enzo Ferrari, meanwhile, had no competitive cars to go against the Germans except the now-outdated

eights and twelves, and he was undoubtedly feeling the strain. But not for long: he was soon named manager for Alfa Corse.

During 1938 several "voiturette" races were staged. The main contenders in this smaller-engine class were the 1500cc British E.R.A.'s and the Maserati 4C and 6C. Before taking up his new job, Ferrari asked the Alfa Romeo board for permission to design and build four 1.5-liter supercharged cars for this series. The board said yes, and sent Gioacchino Colombo, one of the firm's top designers and an Alfa employee since the 1920s, to Modena to work on the project. The result was a beautifully designed car that, with modifications, would bring great prestige to Alfa Romeo after World War II. For this reason, and because it was a Ferrari project, it's worth looking at in detail.

Originally named Alfetta, this car was powered by a straight eight with a 58 x 70mm bore and stroke (2.28 x 2.75 inches) putting displacement at 1497cc (91.3 cid). A light-alloy crankcase was split on the centerline of the crankshaft, which was machined from a chrome steel billet. Dry-sump lubrication was employed, the oil feeding through an external gallery pipe to the seven main bearings and to an eighth bearing immediately adjacent to the flywheel. Oil was drawn from the rear of the crankcase by means of a scavenge pump, and the crankcase base was deeply finned for oil cooling. The block was bolted to the upper face of the crankcase, and comprised two light-alloy castings bolted to each other, each casting with four bores and dry liners. The oil and water pumps, Roots-type supercharger (delivering a boost of 17.6 psi) and single magneto were driven from the front of the engine by a train of gears, as were the twin overhead camshafts. The magneto was strapped to the exhaust side of the camshaft and the supercharger placed centrally on the left of the crankcase. Fuel was

fed via a pump driven from the rear end of the inlet camshaft to a single updraft carburetor positioned directly below the inlet manifold. Exhaust gases were carried via eight pipes to a single pipe that emerged low on the right side, then carried back under the rear suspension adjacent to the wheel. There were two valves per cylinder inclined at 90 degrees. Spark plugs were placed centrally. The water intake pipe was bolted to the cylinder block beneath the exhaust ports. The four-speed gearbox, in unit with the final drive, was located on the rear crossmember. The gearshift gate was mounted to the left side of the cockpit and the oil tank was on the right.

Two parallel rectangular-section steel tubes 4.8 inches deep and 1.38 inches wide made up the frame. Spaced about 18 inches part, they were joined by four crossmembers for added strength. The all-independent suspension featured swing-axle type geometry at the rear, with the wheels located by a single triangular arm fixed to an inclined pivot. A single transverse spring passed under the main axle housing, and was connected by pivot links to the rear hubs. There was also a transverse leaf spring up front, mounted low and connected to the hubs, which were located by trailing arms. Steering was by worm and wheel gear positioned above the clutch housing, and a push-pull rod extended forward under the exhaust system to a bell crank on the front crossmember. The track rods were split in two equal lengths and inclined rearward. Wheelbase was 98.5 inches, and front and rear track were identical at 50 inches. Brakes were hydraulic. The fuel tank, positioned in the tail of the single-seat body, held 37.5 gallons. Both hydraulic and friction shock absorbers were fitted. A distinctive grille sloped back gently to give the Alfetta a low, slim profile, which required the use of two rearview mirrors mounted in fairings separate from the body.

The new 1.5-liter Alfas debuted at Leghorn in July 1938 for the Coppa Ciano. They were driven by Emilio Villoresi (brother of the better-known Luigi), Clemente Biondetti, and Francesco Severi. Villoresi won the 99-mile race at an average speed of 82 mph, with Biondetti taking 2nd and Severi further down the field.

Ferrari quickly became unhappy as Alfa's racing director, no surprise for a man who had been his own master since 1929. By early 1938 he had found it impossible to work with Alfa manager Ugo Gobbato or to have any kind of rapport with chief engineer Wilfredo Ricart. Ferrari resigned and—with Luigi Bazzi, Alberto Massimino, and a few other supporters—went back to Modena to pick up the pieces of his enterprise. But in leaving Alfa, Ferrari had agreed not to build or race any cars that could be considered Alfa competitors for four years. This meant Scuderia Ferrari could not be revived for at least that long. So, he set up a new firm, known initially as Auto Avio Construzioni, to do contract and design work.

Late in December 1939, Ferrari planned to build cars for the 1940 Brescia Grand Prix. In effect, this was to be a revival of Mille Miglia, which had been cancelled by the Italian government because of a serious accident at the 1938 event. The 1940 race was to be organized by the Automobile Club of Brescia, and would be run over a triangular course covering 167 kilometers (103 miles) stretching from Brescia to Cremona to Mantova and back to Brescia. Total race distance was around 1000 miles for what was called the *Gran Premio di Brescia*.

Ferrari had only four months to get ready. Money was short, so he and his team decided to build their contenders around Fiat components. The reason: that firm was offering cash prizes to any class-winning cars using its parts. The Scuderia also needed a

sponsor. They found one in the Marquis Lotario Rangoni Machiavelli, who lived in Modena and had been racing Fiats tuned by Stanguellini. The four-cylinder Fiat 1100 (also known as the 508C) was used as the starting point, and Massimino set about designing the car, which everyone agreed should have an inline eight. A one-piece cylinder block and crankcase was cast by the Calzoni Foundry in Bologna, which also provided a cast aluminum sump and rocker box. Two Fiat 1100 aluminum cylinder heads were placed end to end. The standard valves and rockers were retained, and wet iron liners were inserted in the bores. An oversquare 63 x 60mm (2.48 x 2.36 inch) bore and stroke gave 1496cc (91.3 cid). Two four-cylinder distributors driven by skew gears on the camshaft, (one by cylinder number 3, the other by cylinder number 7) were tried but proved impossible to synchronize. Marelli, the electrical components manufacturer, stepped in with an eight-cylinder distributor driven from the forward skew gear; a tachometer drive was taken from the rear one. The camshaft was designed by Massimino. Using normal Fiat porting, the intake valves were fed by four downdraft Weber 30DR2 carburetors. Two three-branch exhaust manifolds fed into a single pipe running under the car. On a 7.5:1 compression ratio, the new small eight developed 75 bhp at 6000 rpm.

Clutch and gearbox were standard Fiat 1100, as was the chassis. This was a light but rigid cruciform affair of drilled channel section, though it had to be strengthened. Independent front suspension was by enclosed oil-damped coil springs. The light rigid rear axle was mounted on semi-elliptic leaf springs. Steering and brakes were also borrowed from the Fiat 1100, and Borrani wire wheels were used. The alloy envelope body was supplied by Carrozzeria Touring of Milan. Ferrari designated this

new car 815 (for eight cylinders and 1.5-liter displacement). This was cast on the rocker box, and also appeared on a yellow-and-blue badge on the radiator cowling. (It has been suggested that Ferrari felt an impish delight in using these numbers as he, Massimino, and Colombo had conceived the Alfetta 158, a 1.5-liter eight-cylinder car, before leaving Alfa Romeo.) Two cars were constructed in Modena. The first, number 020, would be driven by Machiavelli. The other, 021, was slated for Alberto Ascari, whose father Antonio had been killed in the 1925 French Grand Prix.

The 815s were untouchable at Brescia. Ascari took the lead on the first lap, but soon dropped out due to a broken valve (Massimino suggested it may have been a rocker arm). Machiavelli took over the lead and stretched it to 33 minutes, only to retire near the finish with engine trouble (either a failured roller bearing or, as Enrico Nardi recalled, a broken timing chain). However, he set the fastest lap at over 90 mph, and was timed as high as 108 mph. (Machiavelli's car was eventually sold to a scrap merchant who broke it up, but 021 was taken to Milan by a Mr. Baltracchini, who reportedly entered it for Ascari in its only other race. Around 1954, a collector traced 021 to Lucca and bought it as scrap, though the car was still complete except for its perspex windscreen and one headlamp lens. At the end of April 1956, the restored 021 was exhibited at a trade fair in Modena, and it stll survives today.)

By this time, Italy was enbroiled in World War II, and Ferrari would have to set aside his dreams for a time. But his career was about to enter a new phase, one that would carry his name into posterity on cars with a very special mystique. However future historians may describe him, Ferrari the man is without doubt, an enigmatic figure and very much a living legend.

The Postwar Years: THE FIRST FERRARI CARS

Enrico Nardi had only a small part in the Vettura 815, but he had come to know Enzo Ferrari quite well. During the war years, Nardi introduced Ferrari to an important Torinese machine tool dealer, who put a great deal of work his way—so much, in fact, that Ferrari was able to expand his business to include a factory on the outskirts of Maranello, a suburb of Modena. When hostilities ended, this new facility (which had been bombed during the war a couple of times) had a workforce of nearly 200.

Enzo Ferrari thus emerged from the war years in a strong financial position. He was also the most experienced man in racing, with some 20 years behind him as a driver, administrator, designer, and constructor. Needless to say, he was ready to take up the racing game again as soon as it became feasible.

There is no real clue as to why Ferrari decided on the V-12 engine configuration for the first car to bear his name. However, we do know he was quite fond of this layout, feeling it was ideal not only for racing cars but for road

cars as well. While some Ferrari addicts will tell you that only a V-12 makes a "true" Ferrari, the fact is that the man himself designed or supervised work on four- and six-cylinder inline engines, V-6s, V-8s, and flat-12s. It is also known that Ferrari admired the Packard Twin Six, a car raced by American ace Ralph de Palma. It was a reliable and highly developed machine, but rarely finished in the money, perhaps because it competed on the smaller dirt tracks where a 12-cylinder car couldn't reach its full potential.

The start of the 1947 Circuit of Pescara. Franco Cortese in the number 21 Type 125 went on to win. Number 22 is a Type 815.

Needless to say, Ferrari was fully aware of the V-12 work done by Vittorio Jano for Alfa Romeo, starting with the Tipo A single-seater in 1931, followed by the Tipo C of 1936 and the 1937 Tipo 12C. Even after Jano left to join Lancia, the V-12 tradition carried on at Alfa with the model 312 of 1939, the S10 Prototype GT in 1938, and a V-12 sports/racing car in 1939. With all this there was plenty of available experience on the V-12 layout from which Ferrari could draw. Accordingly, he asked Gioacchini Colombo to design a V-12. As one who had worked with Jano and was fully conversant with this layout, Colombo was only too happy to oblige. For one thing, he felt Jano had been unfairly eased out as chief designer by Alfa management and passed over in favor of Wilfredo Ricart.

Work on the new Ferrari engine did not start until 1946. The first indication it was in the offing came from the Italian magazine *Inter Auto,* which leaked details about it in its November-December issue. In the meantime, Ferrari had engaged a young engineer/draftsman from the Piaggio aircraft and scooter company, Aurelio Lampredi, to work with Colombo. Lampredi had a great feel for engines, but he soon left, feeling the terms of his employment were not satisfactory. However, Ferrari felt he couldn't let Lampredi go, and it wasn't long before he persuaded him to return. Neither engineer would have a long association with Ferrari. Colombo departed in 1948, Lampredi in 1955. But their engine designs would be the basis for virtually all Ferrari's milestone cars in the '50s and '60s, and Colombo's influence extended as far as the early 1970s and the 512S sports/racing car.

As mentioned, many engine configurations have been seen in Ferrari cars, but the most outstanding one is undoubtedly the V-12 with a 60-degree included angle between cylinder banks. Although what we now call the Lampredi engine was an extension of Colombo's original 1946 design, there were many differences between the two units. The former is now referred to as the long-block, the latter as the short-block. The reason has to do with bore spacings, the main distinction between them. The long-block had a 108mm (4.25-inch) spacing between bore centers, the short-block a 90mm (3.54-inch) span.

As important as Colombo and

Lampredi were, other designers and engineers would be equally important in the evolution of Ferrari automobiles. It isn't always easy to single out key individuals for a given model because most worked on project teams and there was a bewildering array of V-12 variations. Still, we can recognize Jano, Fraschetti, Rocchi, Bellentini, Forghieri, and Chitti, and particularly that great

technician Luigi Bazzi, who was always available to help with the impossible.

While Ferrari's first V-12 was developed with grand prix racing in mind, Enzo made it clear that this engine would also power a series of sports cars and *gran turismos,* which he had every intention of building for road use. This made sense for a small firm like Ferrari's because using the same engine with minor changes

Page opposite, above: Peter Whitehead's Type 125S in the paddock at England's Goodwood circuit in 1949. Below: Alberto Ascari hurries the Type 125 to victory in the Daily Express International Trophy race at Silverstone in 1949. This page, above: The Type 125 in GP form in August, 1949. Below: Franco Cortese gives the Type 125 its competition debut at Piacenza in 1947.

for both road and race cars would allow development costs to be spread out over a larger number of units. While it had been intended to build the grand prix cars first, the first Ferraris actually completed were three Type 125 Competizione (125S) models in 1947.

Ferrari issued an imprecise leaflet on the 125S. It showed bore and stroke at 55 x 52.5mm (2.16 x 2.06 inches) giving 1496cc (91.3 cid). A single overhead camshaft per cylinder bank, single plug per cylinder, two distributors or magnetos (probably supplied by Marelli), and three carburetors (either type 30 or type 32 DCF Webers) were other important features. On a compression ratio of 9.5:1, output was 118 bhp at 6800 rpm. The five-speed gearbox was integral with the engine. Front suspension was independent by means of double wishbones and transverse leaf spring while the rear employed a rigid axle suspended on semi-elliptic leaf springs.

Wheelbase was 2420mm (95.3 inches) and front and rear track were both 1240mm (48.8 inches). Three cars were built. Two had full-width bodies by Touring of Milan. The third was fitted with cycle-type fenders and a cigar-shape body.

Two 125S cars were dispatched to Piacenza for a race in May 1947, but the car to be driven by Giuseppe Farina wouldn't start. However, Franco Cortese led the field in the other Ferrari until the last lap, when the aircraft-type centrifugal fuel pump seized. It was a Ferrari's first competition outing. Two weeks later at Rome's Caracalla circuit, Cortese made amends, then went on to win at Vercelli, Vigerano, and Varese, all in June. In July, Tazio Nuvolari, who was not in the best of health, returned to win the sports car class in two events with the 125S.

The Type 159 followed in August. Dimensions on two of the 125 competition engines were changed by boring out to 59mm (2.32 inches) and fitting a new crankshaft that increased stroke to 58mm (2.28) for 1901cc (116 cid). Power was accordingly increased to 125 bhp at 7000 rpm. One of these engines was installed in a full-width 125S

body, the other in the cycle-fender car, which got a new body.

The 166 series appeared in 1948. Initially the Type 159 bore was increased to 60mm (2.36 inches), stroke remaining at 58mm, which gave 1992cc (121 cid). Later, stroke settled at 58.8mm for a capacity of 1995cc (121.7 cid). These cars were called the Spyder Corsa, and had cycle-type fenders. Being open two-seaters, they ran in sports car races and also Formula B (later known as Formula 2). Only 10 were built. The Formula 2 cars were later fitted with single-seat bodies.

Another line of development for the 166 series was a road version that could also be used for competition — the so-called dual-purpose concept that would characterize Ferraris of the '50s and early '60s. The 166 Mille Miglia, for example, was both

This page: The beautiful Type 166 Spyder Corsa was powered by a 2.0-liter V-12. Many ran in Formula 2 events in the late '40s and early '50s. This particular car was owned at one time by American race-car builder Briggs Cunningham. Page opposite: One of the prettiest early Ferraris, the Type 166 Mille Miglia barchetta. Like the Spyder Corsa, this model was every inch a dual-purpose sports car. Luigi Chinetti is shown in the picture at the lower right in the 1949 24 Hours of Le Mans. The barchetta's lovely lines, by Touring of Milan, were later applied to the Type 212 Export chassis.

sports/racing and touring machine. It was apparently built in two series. The first lasted from 1949 to 1951, with Touring of Milan responsible for most of the coachwork, including the attractive and memorable barchetta ("little boat") roadster. The second series ran from late 1952 into 1953, most with spyder bodies styled by Vignale. Out of a total of around 32 built, there were probably 12 or so from both Mille Miglia series with closed coupe (berlinetta) bodies.

Although few were made, the 166 Sport series was probably Ferrari's first attempt at a normal road car. The brochure showed a line drawing of a notchback coupe, probably by Touring, and some bodies could seat rear passengers, albeit in a very confined space. Ferrari's first road car built in any serious numbers, if 37 can be considered serious

production, was the 166 Inter. Touring again did most bodies, though Stabilimenti Farina (not to be confused with Pinin Farina) and Vignale designed and built a few.

Continuing the process inauguarated with the 166, Ferrari next created the Type 195 by increasing the V-12's bore to 65mm (2.56 inches), thus enlarging displacement to 2431cc (148.3 cid). Production of this series was just 24 cars built

between 1950 and 1952. There were both Sport and Inter variations, and coachwork was provided by Ghia and Vignale. There were a few differences between the two models. The Sport had three Weber 32 DCF carburetors for 160-180 bhp at 7000 rpm while the Inter had but one similar instrument, which meant a more modest 130 bhp at 6000 rpm. The Inter also had a longer wheelbase, 2500mm (98.4 inches).

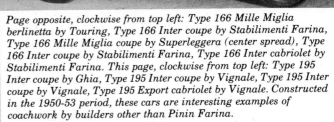

Page opposite, clockwise from top left: Type 166 Mille Miglia berlinetta by Touring, Type 166 Inter coupe by Stabilimenti Farina, Type 166 Mille Miglia coupe by Superleggera (center spread), Type 166 Inter coupe by Stabilimenti Farina, Type 166 Inter cabriolet by Stabilimenti Farina. This page, clockwise from top left: Type 195 Inter coupe by Ghia, Type 195 Inter coupe by Vignale, Type 195 Inter coupe by Vignale, Type 195 Export cabriolet by Vignale. Constructed in the 1950-53 period, these cars are interesting examples of coachwork by builders other than Pinin Farina.

Late in 1950 the important Type 212 was introduced in two versions, the Inter and Export. Production ran into 1953 over 80 Inters and some 24 or 26 Exports. The latter was essentially a competition car for Le Mans, the Tour of Sicily, the Tour de France and the Pan American Road Race. The longer-wheelbase Inter was primarily intended for road use. The 2562cc (156.3-cid) Type 212 engine had a bore and stroke of 68 x 58.8mm (2.67 x 2.31 inches), and was basically the same unit used in earlier Ferraris. The Export had one or three 36 DCF Webers; the early Inters had only one, although later models had three.

In 1950, a group of prominent Mexicans thought up an automobile race that would make the Paris-Peking dash of earlier years seem tame and the Mille Miglia seem small-time. Their race would start on the Guatemala-Mexico border, wend its way north to Mexico City, then on to Juarez near the Texas border, a total of 2125 kilometers (1320 miles). It was not so much the length of the race as the mostly poor roads and mountainous country that were so challenging. This was the fabled

Page opposite, top: The lovely Type 212 Export barchetta takes a curve at Pebble Beach in a "vintage" sports car race in the early '70s. Center and below: A rare Vignale-bodied 212 Export coupe from 1951, photographed in 1968. This page, top and above: Another Vignale creation on the 212 Export chassis. The Export was the competition 212, but this car looks more suited for roadwork than racing. Left: A 1952 cabriolet on the long-wheelbase 212 Inter platform displays typically simple Pinin Farina styling.

Mexican Road Race, officially the "Carrera Panamericana Mexico." A large number of entries from the United States and Mexico competed in the inaugural 1950 event. The winner was Herschel McGriff in an Oldsmobile, followed by a pair of Cadillacs piloted by T. A. Deal and Al Rogers. Next came Piero Taruffi in an Alfa Romeo 6C 2500. In all, there were 47 finishers, remarkable considering the conditions.

Taruffi doubtless described what the race was like to Enzo Ferrari, who decided to field a team for the 1951 running. The reason was logical. Most Ferraris —grand prix cars, sports cars, and *gran turismos,* alike—had been sold in Europe and the United Kingdom. Even though his firm had been in business only a few

2.6-liter Type 212 Vignale coupes. Amazingly, they finished 1st and 2nd. The overall winner was Taruffi, with Luigi Chinetti as co-driver. The runner-up spot went to Alberto Ascari and Luigi Villoresi.

Ferrari continued to support the Mexican Road Race for several years. Cars making the trek included the 225 S (fitted with a 250 MM engine), the

years at this point, Enzo wanted to expand his sales, and there was a lot of money on the other side of the Atlantic. With the publicity of a win in the Mexican Road Race, Enzo knew he could gain at least a foothold in the United States. Accordingly, the firm entered two

Page opposite: The Type 212 Export barchetta differed from its 166 MM predecessor around the nose and in its full-width windscreen. This page: Styling typical of the early '50s graces this 212 Europa coupe designed by Vignale.

appropriately named 340 Mexico coupe, the 250 MM Pinin Farina coupe, 375 MM coupe, 340 MM spyder by Vignale, 500 Mondial, 750 Monza, and 375 Pinin Farina spyder. The drivers were mainly residents of Mexico and Ferrari factory drivers, as well as several Americans who, in later years, would be factory drivers, such as Phil Hill and Richie Ginther.

In some ways, Type 212 marked the end of an era. Up to 1952, Ferrari had turned out only around 200 cars. During the next eleven years, however, total production was on the order 3000-3500, a dramatic rise. The model that put the marque on the road to success as a builder of high-performance automobiles was the 250 series.

With the exception of the first Europa, the 250 series can be conveniently divided into three groups: the competition berlinettas, the sports models, and the GTs. All had the Colombo V-12, similar to the 250 Europa GT powerplant, with single overhead camshaft per cylinder bank, single plug per cylinder, and coil ignition. Except for the GTOs and Testa Rossas, three Weber carburetors were used for all the 250-series models.

37

THE COMPETITION V-12 BERLINETTAS UP TO 3.0 LITERS

A brace of 250 GTOs. Car on the left is the last one built (chassis number 5111), and has non-standard rear tires and wheel wells.

At the Paris Salon in October 1953, Ferrari showed two new *gran turismos*. Both had the Lampredi long-block engine and shared the same basic chassis design. Displacements, though, were different. The 250 Europa was only 2963cc (180.8 cid) compared to 4522cc (275.9 cid) for the 375 America. In every way, these were the largest Ferraris built so far. The reason for the two engine sizes was market requirements. The smaller one was intended for sale in Europe, where taxes in most countries rose sharply on cars with engines larger than 3.0 liters. But there were no such problems to hamper sales in the U.S., hence the larger power unit.

Both the 250 Europa and 375 America were clean and handsome. With them, Pinin Farina set a styling trend that would make him the world's premier automotive designer. About 20 of the 3.0-liter cars were built. These first long-wheelbase Europas had the by-now traditional Ferrari front suspension, with unequal-length A-arms and transverse leaf spring. The frame was a ladder type made up of welded steel tubes. A second series of Europas bore the GT suffix, but these cars had the 2953cc (180.2-cid) Colombo short-block engine and a 2600mm (102.3-inch) wheelbase versus 2800mm (110.2 inches) for the earlier cars.

International sports car racing made great strides after World War II. By 1955, the cars eligible

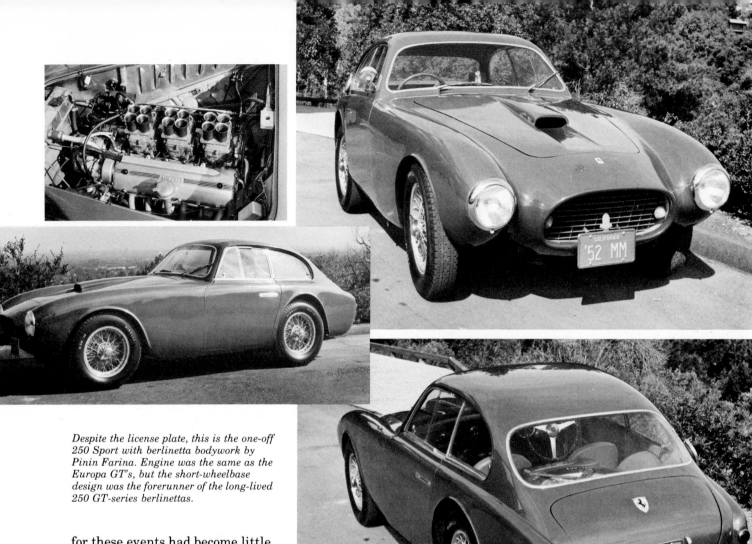

Despite the license plate, this is the one-off 250 Sport with berlinetta bodywork by Pinin Farina. Engine was the same as the Europa GT's, but the short-wheelbase design was the forerunner of the long-lived 250 GT-series berlinettas.

for these events had become little more than grand prix racers with two-seat enclosed bodywork. This fact was brought home tragically with Pierre Levegh's ghastly and disastrous accident at the 1955 Le Mans 24 Hours. There was an immediate call in racing circles for a return to a more traditional format with specifications closer to those of production sports cars. For the 1956 season, the Federation Internationale de l'Automobile (FIA, the governing body) established specific classes for *gran turismos*. As Ferrari had been building berlinettas for the major long-distance events since 1950, he was not unprepared for the new regulations.

All this led to the 250 Sport (or 250/S as shown on the factory data sheet). This was a one-off berlinetta (chassis number 1056 ET) with the same 3.0-liter capacity as the Europa GT but a shorter 2400mm (94.4-inch) wheelbase. Perhaps Ferrari was already thinking of the

short-wheelbase dual-purpose car that came on stream in 1959. The 250 Sport, in turn, sired a new series of long-wheelbase berlinettas with bodywork by Pinin Farina. Construction was again by Scaglietti, who by now had a virtual monopoly on building Ferrari bodies. It was obvious that Scaglietti had design ideas of his own. For example, he felt that some Pinin Farina shapes were a little too sharp, so he often rounded off the lines creating softer forms with a hint of voluptuousness.

The competition berlinettas can be classified into three main types: the long- and short-wheelbase cars and, the

most sought after, the GTOs.

The 250 long-wheelbase berlinetta made its racing debut in December 1955, when the Marquis de Portago won at Nassau. This was followed early in 1956 when Belgians Olivier Gendebien and Jacques Wascher won their class in the Tour of Sicily (placing 4th overall) and in the Mille Miglia (finishing 5th overall). Later that year, the model became known as the Tour de France, although the name was never officially used by the factory.

The Tour de France competition literally took place around the perimeter of France, a race and rally some 3600 miles long. It

included a variety of special stages: six track races held on major circuits, two hillclimbs, even a drag race. De Portago and Nelson won five of the six circuit races in their lwb berlinetta, and were overall winners of the 1956 Tour, the fifth one held. From then until production of the series ended in 1959 the long-wheelbase berlinettas carried the Tour de France nickname.

The cars can be distinguished from one another by the louvers on their rear quarter roof panels. Those built in 1956 had none. On the '57s the factory cut in 14 louvers decreasing in depth front to rear. For 1958 there were three, and 1959 cars had but a single louver. In all years, three Weber 36 DCL3 barburetors were used, as was a four-speed all-synchromesh transmission in unit with the engine via a single dry-plate clutch. On a compression ratio of 9.57:1, power from the V-12 engine was an impressive 260 bhp at 7000 rpm. To keep weight down aluminum was used for major body panels.

The Tour de France berlinettas were very successful throughout the 1956 season. Many non-factory teams raced them, including Camillo Luglio, who notched five 1sts and two 2nds in

A later evolution of the basic "Tour de France" style, this 1958 berlinetta was used by the late Bill Harrah as a daily driver when new.

his lightweight Zagato-bodied car. For 1957, Scaglietti made a few minor modifications to the coachwork, but retained the cold-air scoop on the hood. Rear windows were made smaller and, as already noted, louvers

The 1957 250 GT "Tour de France" berlinetta.

appeared on the quarter panels. Once more the long-wheelbase cars showed their superiority, scoring a 1-2-3-4-5 victory in the

Above and right: This 1959 250 GT "Tour de France" was used primarily for racing, though there are few clues outside compared to the Harrah car on the previous page. Below: Only seven of the "Interim" long-wheelbase berlinettas were built. Styling previewed the swb of 1959-62.

12-hour Reims event. Gendebien and Paul Frere won outright at an average of 104 mph, and set the lap record with a remarkable 115 mph. Another big win was a 1-2-3 finish in the 1957 Tour de France in September. The 1958 season would be no less successful.

While these cars were used extensively in GT racing, they were also docile and tractable as road cars. For this reason, the Tour de France must be included among the ranks of "classic" Ferraris. All told, 85 of the lwb berlinettas were produced. Those with the Tour de France designation are very sought-after and command accordingly steep prices today. However, it's surprising to realize that the short-wheelbase cars that followed are even more highly prized, even though their competition record did not approach that of the long-wheelbase models.

In 1959 three new berlinetta models appeared. Again, all were Pinin Farina creations built by Scaglietti. The first looked more like a road car than a competition machine, with uncovered headlamps surrounded by chrome rims. The second departed from the 1956-58 concept. Its contours were more rounded, the hood sloped down low between the front fenders, its grille was tucked under, and headlamps were set out at the front of the fenders.

Rear overhang was also much shorter. Glass area was increased by replacing the rear quarter panel with a small window, and vent wings were added to the doors. (All these extra windows did nothing to enhance appearance.) This second design was built on the long-wheelbase

Though not as successful in competition as the long-wheelbase berlinettas, the Pinin Farina-styled 250 GT short-wheelbase coupes are more highly prized today. Timeless lines and ferocious performance are but two of the many reasons.

1958 platform, but there were no modifications to either chassis or engine. Seven of these so-called "Interim" berlinettas were built (chassis numbers 1377 to 1523). Their main significance is in the styling, which would be carried over to the next production model, the 250 short-wheelbase

berlinetta. Otherwise, the Interim (again a nickname and not recognized by the factory) is dismissed out of hand by most Ferrarists.

It's interesting to note a cutaway drawing of an Interim 250 that appeared in a French auto publication. It showed a

Testa Rossa 12-port engine with six twin-choke Weber carburetors and the spark plugs located outboard of the heads (Colombo engines usually had the plugs inboard). Disc brakes were also fitted. It can only be assumed that at least one of the Interim cars had these mechanical features. Once again a long-wheelbase car, an Interim 250, won the September 1959 Tour de France, with Gendebien/Bianchi as co-drivers. This made four consecutive victories for Ferrari in the series. The Interim also

Three variations on the 250 GT swb theme: the "production" version (upper right), a competition model with custom "twin-nostril" grille (above), and a special Pinin Farina-bodied example (right and far right) with curious rear deck fins.

competed at Le Mans, taking 4th and 6th places overall.

The Paris Salon in October ushered in the third 1959 berlinetta design. Engine and chassis were basically as for previous 250 models, but wheelbase was cut to 2400mm (94.5 inches). This was the start of the 250 short-wheelbase berlinetta line, 250 swb for short. There can be little doubt that the styling here was the most pleasing yet seen on a Ferrari. An evolution from the short-tailed body on one Interim 250, it lended itself readily to both competition and road use, and the new model would ultimately fill both roles. Most of the road-going swbs had steel bodies with aluminum doors, hood, and trunklid, but there was a competition version with all-aluminum coachwork.

The well-proven Colombo engine again powered this new member of the 250 series, but used Testa Rossa-type cylinder heads with individual ports and coil valve springs. And, as on that one Interim car, plug location was outboard. Apart from a more civilized interior, the "street" 250 swb also had a milder engine than the competition model, with three

Weber 40 DCL6 or 36 DCL3 carburetors giving output of between 220 and 240 bhp at 7000 rpm. The race version was fed by three 40 DCL6, 46 DCL3 or 46 DCF3 Webers and, on a 9.0:1 compression ratio, its output was between 260 and 280 bhp at 7000 rpm.

Due to its body and wheelbase alterations, the 250 swb was not immediately certified by the FIA. This meant the new car would be unable to compete in the GT class, and would have to run instead in an open class against sports cars. A good many 250 swbs were entered in the 1960 Sebring 12-hour race, including several driven by Americans. Running out of class, the cars notched 4th (Hugus/Pabst), 6th (Sturgis/D'Orey) and 7th

(Arents/Kimberly) overall. Then, the FIA homologated the swb in time for the annual 24 Hours of Le Mans in June, and several were entered along with a number of long-wheelbase cars. Ferrari swept the board, taking 1st, 2nd, 4th, 5th, 6th, and 7th places. Fernand Tavano and Loustel drove their swb to 4th overall and won the GT class at an average speed of 105 mph. Similar cars took 5th, 6th, and 7th overall. The outright winner was the Gendebien/Frere TR 60 Testa Rossa. The 250 swb also continued Ferrari's domination of the Tour de France, taking the first three places in the 1960 event.

The swb was a winner, whether in the hands of factory drivers or privateers. Few design changes

were made from 1959 until production ended in 1962. Side louvers were added to the front and rear fenders for 1960, and vent windows appeared a bit later.

No other marque but Ferrari seemed capable of producing truly dual-purpose cars like the 250 berlinettas of the '50s. All were good-looking machines capable of superb performance, which earned them an outstanding record in races, rallies, and hillclimbs. These cars and the GTOs that followed showed the world what real racing was all about, and many enthusiasts would argue that, in the years they were active, racing was at its grandest and most romantic. They represent what Ferrari lovers consider the true Ferrari, a

car for all seasons.

While most 250-series bodies were styled by Pinin Farina and built by Scaglietti, Carrozzeria Bertone also did design work for Ferrari, if only occasionally. The first was a cabriolet on the 166 Inter chassis in 1950. The next one, a good-looking coupe on the 250 GT chassis, wasn't exhibited until much later, 1960, when it was shown at the Geneva Salon. The most recent Bertone-bodied Ferrari was the production 308 GT4 2+2, which appeared at the Paris Salon in 1973. Before this, however, came an attractive one-off coupe built on a 250 swb chassis. Following the front-end treatment of the Formula 1 and sports/racing cars of 1961-62, this had twin nostril-like air intakes, which set it apart from all other

Top: The first production GTO seen in early 1962 lacked a rear spoiler; all later cars had it. Above: Bertone styled this striking 250 GT swb berlinetta for the 1966 European auto show season.

250-series designs. Horizontal louvers were set into the front and rear fenders, and the roof swept gracefully down to the tail.

The last of the series-built competition berlinettas is the one most favored by Ferrarists. Today, these cars command astronomical prices on the collector market, though they don't come up for sale very often. Of course we're talking about the Type 250 GTO, introduced by Enzo Ferrari himself at his annual press conference in February 1962.

The GTO's genesis was Le

Mans 1961 and a lightweight prototype berlinetta with Pinin Farina coachwork derived from the Superfast II show car and built on a 2400mm (94.5-inch) wheelbase. An engine similar to that of the 250 Testa Rossa was installed, with six Weber 38 DCN carburetors good for 300 bhp at 7500 rpm. Fernand Tavano and Giancarlo Baghetti shared the drive, and were running in 7th when engine problems put them out of the race during the 13th hour. The same car ran in the Daytona 3-hour race in February 1962, and took 4th overall in the hands of Stirling Moss. This car was the direct predecessor of the GTO. Despite the prototype's low, sleek lines, its aluminum bodywork was prone to front-end lift at high speed. After further testing a longer, lower nose was developed, with two vertical slots on the front fenders to allow underhood air to escape. The extra work also resulted in a new tail, higher than the prototype's

and with an almost Kamm-type cutoff giving it a squarish appearance. This was supposed to reduce rear overhang (and also weight) without affecting aerodynamics, provided the roof slope was minimal. The first production GTO had no rear spoiler. However, one was added when the car made its race debut at Sebring in March 1962, and would be a feature of all

subsequent models. This car was co-driven by Phil Hill and Olivier Gendebien, who finished 2nd overall and 1st in the GT class, an auspicious start for the new model.

The GTO chassis was quite similar to that of the swb berlinetta. Front suspension was still by means of unequal length A-arms and coil springs concentric with the tubular shock

absorbers. Engineer Giotto Bizzarrini had thought of using coil springs instead of semi-elliptics for the live rear axle, but feared the FIA might not homologate the GTO if any drastic changes were made. Thus, he used coils around the rear shocks only as "compensators." Longitudinal location for the back axle was, as before, by twin parallel trailing arms. The frame was still constructed of welded steel tubing.

The GTO engine was similar to the Testa Rossa unit, but with dry-sump lubrication and a displacement of 2953cc (180 cid). Carburetion was by six Weber 38DCN twin-choke downdraft units. Power was taken through a single dry-plate clutch and a five-speed all-synchromesh gearbox with direct-drive fifth gear. Disc brakes were used all around. The GTO was about 6.6 inches longer and 3.5 inches lower than the 250 swb.

Scarlatti and Ferraro drove a GTO in the Targa Florio in May 1962, winning the GT class and finishing 4th overall. The following week, at Silverstone in England, Mike Parkes placed 1st, with American Masten Gregory taking 2nd. Next, Ferrari entered a GTO prototype using the 400 Superamerica 4.0-liter (244-cid) power unit for the Nurburgring 1000km race in May. Parkes and Willy Mairesse did the driving, and finished 2nd overall. Two "standard" GTOs were eliminated, and it was left to a 1960 25 short-wheelbase berlinetta to win the GT class. At the important Le Mans race, a GTO won in class and was 2nd overall. GTOs also finished 3rd and 6th, the latter wheeled by Americans Bob Grossman and stock-car ace Fireball Roberts.

The original Le Mans prototype from the year before took the flag in 9th position, driven by Americans Ed Hugus and George Reed. The GTOs continued their winning ways, although they conceded the September Tour de France, where Ferrari won for the seventh straight year thanks to a 250 swb. However, they annihilated the opposition in the 1000 Kilometers of Paris at Montlhery in October.

At his annual press conference in December 1962, Enzo Ferrari said it was his intention to build only a few more GTOs because he considered them too fast and too unwieldy for all except the top-line drivers. Up to then, 25 had been built, including two 4.0-liter examples. Another 10 would be built in 1963, including

The most romantic, the most charismatic dual-purpose sports car of all time, the 250 GTO was quite successful as an endurance racer and garnered a legion of fans whose number seems to grow ever larger as time passes. The car pictured above now resides in England and is one of the earlier examples, as indicated by the two vertical slots in the front fenders. The car on the left also lives in England and belongs to enthusiast Nick Mason. It's shown hammering around the Goodwood circuit in 1978 at a Ferrari Owners' Club meet. The GTO chassis was quite similar to that of the 250 GT swb berlinetta, and its engine was derived from the 3.0-liter Testa Rossa V-12. Three prototypes with the 4.0-liter 400 Superamerica powerplant were also constructed. Total GTO production was a mere 39 cars, and this rarity is only part of the reason why this remains the one Ferrari model virtually every Ferrariphile would love to own.

Above: A British-registered first-series GTO (chassis no. 3527 GT) from late 1962.
Right: The "Breadvan" was the most famous of three "pseudo" GTOs built privately.

one 4.0-liter. As noted elsewhere, Ferrari's numbering system allocated even chassis numbers for competition cars and odd numbers for road cars. All the GTOs were given odd numbers, which suggests the factory throught of them more as tourers than racers.

Up to 1964 the GTO had little competition on the track. Although the lightweight E-Type Jaguars could have been a threat, it was the Shelby Cobras that proved the real menace. Created by ex-Ferrari racer Carroll Shelby, the Cobra was a British A.C. Ace powered by the reliable American Ford 289-cid ohv V8. The Anglo-American hybrid proved a worthy opponent, finishing only a few points behind Ferrari in the 1964 Manufacturers' Championship with 78.3 points to Maranello's 84.6.

Ferrari, meanwhile, had concocted something new, the mid-engine 250 LM (Le Mans). This was a closed version of the 250 P sports/racing prototype that had made its debut in November at Monza. Ferrari had hoped the LM would be approved by the CSI (Commission Sportive Internationale, an arm of the FIA) for homologation, but the request was turned down as too few cars had been built to satisfy the 100-unit minimum. So, for the 1964 campaign there was a Series II GTO using the original chassis but with noticeably changed bodywork. Instead of the small air

intakes on the nose and elliptical grille there was now a smooth hood and a wide, oval mesh grille. The windshield was sharply raked, almost a wraparound. The rear roofline was more upright, the previous pure fastback being replaced by a vertical backlight framed by "flying buttress" sail panels. The whole car was stubby compared to the "Mark I" GTO (4.3 inches shorter, 2.3 inches wider, 2.1 inches lower), but made

continued on page 65

Type 166 Corsa Spyder

The Type 166 Corsa Spyder equipped with cycle-type fenders for sports car racing. A mere 10 were built.

Type 166 Inter

TJ 331·289

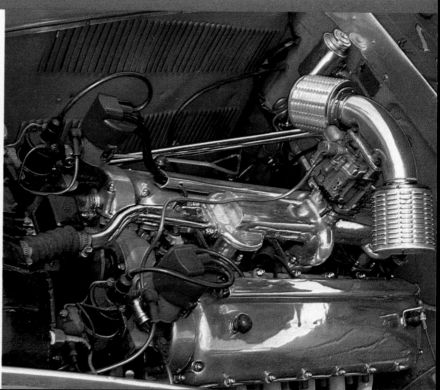

This Type 166 Inter is in original condition, down to its steel disc wheels by Borrani, a firm better known for its wire wheels. The Inter was the first Ferrari designed as a road car. Some 37 were made. Vignale and Stabilimenti bodywork was available in addition to the body by Touring of Milan shown here.

Type 166MM
& Type 195 Sport

Above: The dual-purpose Type 166MM (Mille Miglia) built for competition and road use. It was produced in barchetta and coupe form and in two series. Below: the Type 195 Sport produced between 1950 and 1952. Bodywork was supplied by both Ghia and Vignale.

Type 212 Inter
& Export

Introduced in 1950, the Type 212 was sold in two versions, the Inter and the Export. The former was a road car, the latter a competition model for long-distance racing. On the page opposite is the barchetta built by Superleggera. Above and below is the Inter cabriolet by Vignaler, one of the most elegant touring cars ever designed.

Type 340MM

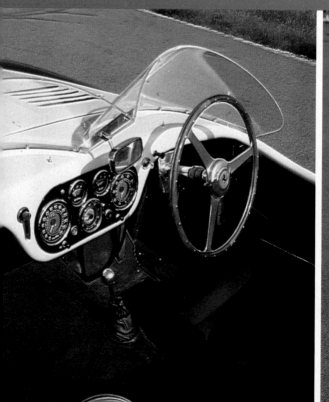

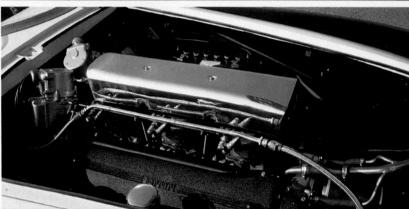

In 1953, Ferrari introduced the 340MM, which had the long-block Lampredi engine and was used for long-distance racing. It was successful in competition. The example pictured here was built for an American, and has been restored to its original black-and-white color scheme by the present owner, who still races it.

Type 340 Mexico
& Type 375MM

Above: The Type 340 Mexico was purpose-built for the gruelling Carrera Panamericana races of the '50s, hence its name. A spyder and three berlinettas were built. Below: The powerful and brutish-looking 4.5-liter 375MM. Both berlinetta and spyder body styles were available.

JLS 513

410 Superamerica

The 410 Superamerica was a replacement for the 375 America. The car shown here, styled by Ghia, was recently located in the U.S. It bears a close resemblance to Ghia's Chrysler "Dart" show car of 1957, reflecting Ferrari's desire to break into the U.S. market at the time. The 410 SA was built on both long- and short-wheelbase chassis. Total production was 36 in all.

250 Testa Rossa

In 1957, Ferrari was interested in designing a car suitable for the 1958-61 World Sports Car Championship series. The result was the superlative 250 Testa Rossa ("red head"), a sports car with elegant body styling. It had a lifespan of four years, with various modifications to bodywork and mechanicals over the years. It won the championship in 1958, 1960, and 1961.

410 Superfast

Another of the Type 410 Super-americas. This car has scored a number of wins in concours events in the United Kingdom.

its presence felt just like its predecessor. But Ferrari was beginning to lose interest, believing the 250 LM should take over from the GTO in premier endurance events. At his press conference that December Ferrari announced he would not compete in GT racing in 1965. Nevertheless, GTOs would still be very much a power for a few more years in the hands of privateers. In all, 39 GTOs were built, including the three 4.0-liter specials.

There were also three "pseudo" GTOs constructed in 1962 on the short-wheelbase 250 GT chassis. They were the brainchild of designer Piero Drogo's Modena Sports Cars Company. Giotto Bizzarini, who had been responsible for chassis development on the 250 swb and GTO, helped Giorgio Neri and Luciano Bonacini with the mechanical and technical work. The best known of the three was the "breadvan" (chassis no. 2819) built for Count Volpi's Scuderia Republica Venezia. Originally an aluminum-bodied 250 swb berlinetta, it was acquired by Olivier Gendebien in 1961 for the Tour de France (with co-driver Lucien Bianchi, he finished 2nd behind Mairesse/Berger in another 250 swb). The rebodied car had a lower nose, similar in profile to the GTO's but with twin nostrils, and had a clear plastic bubble at the back of the hood to cover the carburetors. The breadvan got its name because of its roofline, which went straight back without any slope. This terminated in a high, truncated tail with a large rear window (complete with wiper) filling over half the back area. The effect was very much like a panel truck. This car raced four times in 1962. Its highest placing was a 3rd in the 1000 kilometers of Montlhery.

The second pseudo GTO bore no resemblance to the real thing. It, too, was originally a 250 swb (chassis no. 2735 GT), and was owned by Rob Walker, one of the last independents to field a grand prix team. Usually driven by

Stirling Moss, this car had a checkered career that numbered five 1st place finishes in relatively minor events during 1961. It was then sold to Chris Kerrison, who campaigned it with little success through 1964.

A third GTO-like car was also based on the 250 swb (chassis no. 2053). The original car was owned by a C. Toselli and raced by him without distinction in 1960. He then sold it to Ecurie Francorchamps. It crashed at Le Mans in 1962, and was then bought by Equipe Nationale

Top: The Series II GTO looked considerably different than earlier models. Above: A Series I GTO in action circa 1963.

Belge and sent to Drogo for a rebuild. The result was really quite ugly (especially the low, pointy, twin-nostril front), but the car managed two respectable placings in long-distance events, a 4th at Spa-Francorchamps and a 5th overall at Nurburgring. In the hands of M. Remordu it won four minor events in 1963, but was totally wrecked at Spa in 1964.

THE V-12 SPORTS/ RACING CARS UP TO 3.0 LITERS

During 1952, Enzo Ferrari decided to develop the short-block Colombo engine further even though the Lampredi 4.5-liter unit could be used in sports car competition. He felt that a smaller-engine car would be handier on some tracks, and therefore more acceptable to his racing customers, than the bulkier and more powerful machines of the day. The 250 Sport was the prototype for a new series of berlinettas and spyders introduced in 1953. These were designated 250 MM in honor of Bracco's victory with the 250 Sport in the Mille Miglia.

Generally speaking, the new design followed contemporary Ferrari practice. Unequal-length A-arms with a transverse leaf spring comprised the independent front suspension, and a live rear axle on semi-elliptic springs was located by twin parallel trailing arms. Drive was via a multiple-disc racing clutch

around with inline four- and six-cylinder engines. Even so, there were signs that Enzo was unhappy over the idea of possibly abandoning the V-12 as the mainstay of his competition cars. The 250 Monza was, therefore, very much a stopgap. Only four

Enzo's emphasis on his larger-displacement cars, a bias that would often leave designs that might have evolved into good racers neglected and underdeveloped.

The 250 Monza appeared in the mid-'50s at a time when the factory was playing

Above: The fabulous 250 Testa Rossa with the early "pontoon" or "sponson" bodywork by Pinin Farina. Below: The rare and very desirable 250 Mille Miglia berlinetta.

through a non-synchromesh five-speed gearbox on racing models or a four-speed all-synchro transmission on road models. The frame was the usual welded tubular-steel affair with the oval-section main tubes forming an X and subsidiary members extending to the edges of the body. Coachwork for the spyders was designed by Vignale, the closed cars by Pinin Farina.

The 250 MM did not fare well during the 1953 season, with most events going to the big-block 340 MM and the new 375 MM. Phil Hill won with his 250 MM at Pebble Beach in April, but suffered rear axle failure in two subsequent events. The model's lack of success probably reflects

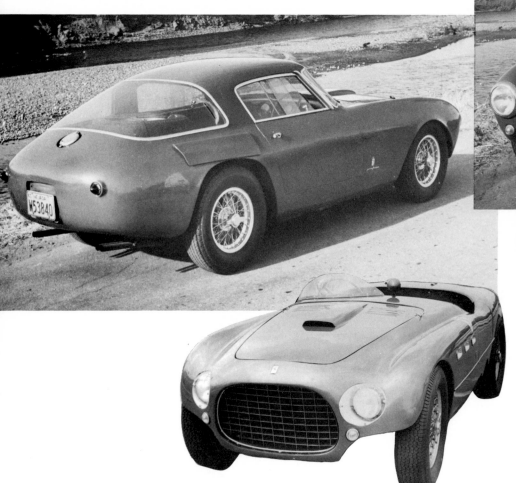

were produced. It used the 2953cc (180.2-cid) Colombo engine from the 250 MM installed in a chassis believed to be the same as that of the 500 Mondial and 750 Monza four-cylinder cars. The rear suspension employed De Dion-type geometry, and the four-speed gearbox was in unit with the engine. All four cars were spyders, two designed by Pinin Farina and two by Scaglietti. (The former carried chassis numbers 0420 M and 0466 M; the latter were 0432 M and 0442 M.) Apart from this, little else is known about the 250 Monza.

In 1957, Enzo Ferrari was concerned with the 1958 World Sports Car Championship, which would have a 3.0-liter displacement limit. Since his 3.0-liter V-12 cars were still the ones to beat in GT racing, he decided that, with further development, this engine could be

This page: The 250 MM berlinetta by Pinin Farina (top left and right) and the Vignale-styled spyder (above). Center and page opposite: The romantic 250 Testa Rossa, one of Ferrari's most successful sports/racers. Car at lower right has the later "aerodynamic" bodywork.

a winner in the sports car classes, too. The result was a new model designated 250 Testa Rossa ("red head") because of the distinctive red finish used on its cam covers. Why this color was chosen is anybody's guess, but one reason may be that Ferrari liked the name. He had already used it on the four-cylinder 2.0-liter 500 TR and 500 TRC built during 1956-57 for customer use.

The first prototype 250 Testa Rossa (chassis 0666) was seen in competition at the Nurburgring 1000km in May 1957. Ferrari had also entered a 335S and a 315S (plus a 250 GT berlinetta), and the TR bore a close resemblance

to these cars. Gendebien put the TR 6th on the grid, but Masten Gregory and Marolli drove it in the race. At one point it was running 4th, but ended up in 10th place. For Le Mans a second prototype (chassis 0704) with a 3117cc (190.2-cid) engine was entered (along with the Nurburgring car, which didn't start, though). Styling changes comprised front fenders cut away behind the wheels to allow a greater flow of cool air to the front brakes, and a low nose that jutted out further than the fenders. This treatment became known as the "pontoon" or "sponson" body, and was a most exciting and unusual design. Gendebien and Maurice Trintignant were the drivers. Although lying 2nd overall at one

stage, the new Testa Rossa had to retire due to piston failure, as did other Ferraris fitted with the new experimental pistons. Both Testa Rossas ran in other events before ending the season at Caracas, where they proved reliable by finishing 3rd and 4th behind their larger-capacity 335S teammates.

At his November 1957 press conference, Ferrari introduced two 2953cc (180.2-cid) Testa Rossa models. There would be one version for the factory team and another for private customers. Both would have six twin-choke Weber 38 DCN carburetors and 9:1 compression ratio, good for 300 bhp at 7200 rpm. Both would also share a 2350mm (92.5-inch) wheelbase, ladder-type frame, and independent front suspension with unequal-length A-arms and coil springs. At the rear, however, the factory cars would employ either the De Dion/transverse leaf spring arrangement as on the 290 MM or a live axle, while customer cars would have only the latter. All cars would have drum brakes. One other area of difference related to driving position: factory cars could be either right- or left-hand drive; customer cars would be left-hand drive only.

The 1958 championship races were scheduled for Buenos Aires, Sebring, the Targa Florio, Nurburgring, Le Mans, and Goodwood. All would be 1000km events. Ferrari was in a strong position, and only Porsche and Aston Martin were expected to

mount any serious challenge. At Buenos Aires and Sebring, the 250 TRs placed 1st and 2nd, with the Phil Hill/Peter Collins car winning on each occasion. A new envelope body replaced the previous pontoon style, which had proved aerodynamically unsuitable, for the Targa Florio in May, when Luigi Musso and Gendebien led from start to finish. Ferrari duly won the championship.

For 1959 the TR showed a few changes from its '58 specification. Enzo Ferrari was at last "converted" to disc brakes (he had first tried them when he removed the Dunlop units from Peter Collins' personal 250 GT spyder and had them fitted to a grand prix car). The frame was lightened, and the transmission and limited-slip differential were coupled together at the back as a transaxle. The telescopic shock absorbers were relocated inside the coil springs, and the engine was now offset to the left. The driver still sat on the right in a newly styled body designed by Pinin Farina and constructed by Fantuzzi (Scaglietti was, for a change, completely occupied — with other Ferrari coachwork). An important internal modification was adoption of coil valve springs to replace the hairpin type that had been a feature of both the Colombo and Lampredi engines up to this point. Ferrari was taking his cue from American racing experience, because the coil springs allowed higher rpm. The Forged-True Piston Company in Pasadena provided these springs, and would continue to do so for a number of years.

Engine problems beset the TRs during the '59 season, and after Le Mans dry-sump lubrication was adopted. The last race, held at the Goodwood circuit in England, saw the Stirling Moss/Carroll Shelby Aston Martin DBR1 take the checkered flag, with Jo Bonnier's Porsche 2nd. Ferrari had missed winning the cup.

The Testa Rossa was further altered for what would be a close 1960 season. The new TR/60 and TRI/60 (the 'I' stood for independent suspension all round) had their engines placed lower in the chassis, a benefit of the switch to dry-sump lubrication, and were given a new four-speed all-indirect transmission. Some cars ran with irs, but some had the De Dion rear end as Ferrari was not convinced an independent layout would prove effective. At the Buenos Aires 1000km race, the leading Birdcage Maserati didn't last due to rear axle failure, leaving Phil Hill and Richie Ginther to score an easy 1-2 victory in their TRI/60s.

The ensuing championship events—Sebring, the Targa Florio and Nurburgring— brought no joy to Enzo, although his cars placed high and scored valuable points. So it all came down to Le Mans, where Ferrari had to win to regain the championship lost so narrowly the year before. He did it with stunning results. The grid was packed with Ferraris. The Hill/Von Trips TRI/60 ran out of gas near the end and stopped too far away from the pits to refuel. But the Frere/Gendebien and Ricard Rodriguez/Andre Pilette cars placed 1st and 2nd, and short-wheelbase berlinettas finished 4th, 5th, 6th, and 7th. Only the Roy Salvadori/Jim Clark Aston Martin prevented a clean sweep. Ferrari had won the championship a second time.

Manufacturers and drivers alike were incensed at one FIA regulation for 1960 that decreed higher windshields and even windshield wipers. The bigger windshields collected more insects and dust, and the wipers were quite ineffective at racing speeds. Perhaps for this reason, Ferrari made further body changes to the Testa Rossa for the 1961 season. Carlo Chiti arrived from Alfa Romeo, and went to work on a new body designed with the aid of a wind tunnel. He knew

This page: The 250 Testa Rossa prototype in 1957, probably at Le Mans. Page opposite, above: 250 TR/61 (chassis no. 0792) displays distinctive "twin-nostril" front. Below: Pinin Farina's Spyder Competizione show special appears to be based on the long-wheelbase 250 GT Cabriolet.

this was the only way to improve aerodynamics not only on the 250 TRs but also on the newer mid-engine sports/racing cars then coming on the scene. As a result, the new TRI/61 had a low-profile nose and a higher rear end with a spoiler and a Kamm-type tail. The spoiler helped prevent exhaust fumes from inundating the cockpit at slower speeds and also aided high-speed stability at some expense at the top end. Two of the newly bodied cars appeared at Sebring with twin-nostril noses, the third with a 1960-style nose. Among other Ferraris entered was the new mid-engine V-6 246 SP, making its race debut. The

250 TRs took the first four places, with the Hill/Gendebien team taking the checkered flag. The 246 SP won the Targa Florio. A Maserati won at Nurburgring, but Ferraris took the next four places to score useful championship points. Le Mans again saw a Ferrari sweep — a 1-2-3 finish headed by Hill/Gendebien. This gave Ferrari an overwhelming lead in the points standings. Ferrari clinched the championship when Scuderia Centro Sud won the Pescara 4-hour race with a TRI/61 loaned for the occasion. Ferrari was now riding a 3 for 4 win streak.

By now, though, the 250 TR was nearing the end of its useful

competition life. Its last important outing was Sebring 1962, where Scuderia Republica de Venezia won with a TRI/62 driven by Bonnier/Bianchi.

A 4.0-liter prototype class was included for Le Mans 1962. Ferrari seemed disinterested, but in the end he just couldn't resist having a go at it. His contender was an amalgam of the Testa Rossa chassis and a modified 400 Superamerica engine with six twin-choke Webers. Two of these hybrids were fielded, a spyder and a berlinetta. The former was driven by Hill/Gendebien, and this team scored its third Le Mans win. It was in this race that the new 250 GTO first appeared, finishing 1st in class and 2nd overall.

After this, the front-engine layout, as far as Ferrari was concerned, was finished as a factory racer. Enzo was at last convinced that placing the engine behind the driver was the coming thing for racing and sports/racing cars. Though there would be other front-engine Ferraris, they would run only in the *gran turismo* classes.

As noted earlier, many of Ferrari's first semi-race models could also be driven on normal roads. Yet for all practical purposes, they really weren't that suitable for what most people would consider daily use, certainly not for shopping or commuting chores. Perhaps the closest thing to a practical "street" Ferrari in the early years was the 212 Inter. There was also the 166 Sport, a notchback coupe with only very limited space in the rear. The first of Ferrari's true road cars was the 250 Europa. This was followed by the 250 Europa GT with the 2953cc (180.2-cid) short-block V-12, an engine that would be the mainstay of both competition and *gran turismo* models for many years. It seems that the Europa GT was conceived as a rival for the Mercedes-Benz 300SL, but it was left to the later 250 GT berlinettas to make the Ferrari

name famous throughout the world.

At the March 1956 Geneva Salon, Pinin Farina displayed a prototype coupe and Carrozzeria Boano displayed a cabriolet, both on the 250 GT chassis. It was suggested by the Italian press that both would eventually be offered for sale. They were, but interestingly Boano ended up

doing the coupe, which was shown, with minor changes, in production form at the Paris Salon that October. Carrozzeria Boano had been established in 1954 by Mario Boano, his son Gianpaolo, and Luciano Pollo. The firm built between 70 and 80 Ferraris to the 1956 design. In 1957, Mario Boano moved over to Fiat, and his firm was taken over

THE V-12 GRAN TURISMOS UP TO 3.0 LITERS

by his son-in-law, Ezio Ellena, and Pollo. A revised coupe was drawn up for 1958, to be built by the same company but renamed for Ellena. Around 50 of these coupes were completed. As the Ellena coupe had a slightly higher roofline than the 1956-57 Boano design, the latter is sometimes referred to as the low-roof, the former the high-roof. The Boano had side vent windows and, on some examples, a reversed gate for the four-speed transmission. The Ellena model did away with the vent windows and reverted to a standard shift gate.

These were the most comfortable Ferraris yet, and also had more luggage room than previous models. Their panel and general trim quality was superb. A heater was standard equipment, but there were no extras listed. Their simple slab-sided styling still looks elegant today, though bumpers were more for decoration than protection. Both coupes used a good many proprietary components, such as door latches, windshield wipers, and window mechanisms, supplied by Fiat and Alfa Romeo. This meant some replacement parts were readily available and comparatively inexpensive for an upper-class car. Surprisingly, neither coachbuilder signed its creations with identifying script or emblems.

Page opposite: The 250 Europa. This page, above: An unusual 250 GT Europa by Vignale. Below: The 250 GT Spyder California.

During the winter of 1957-58, prototypes emerged for a new-style Pinin Farina coupe on the 250 chassis. The first of these was shown publicly in June 1958. Pinin Farina had been supplying Ferrari bodies since 1952 but in relatively small numbers. Production of this new design would run until 1960 over some 350 units, the largest volume for a single Ferrari model up to that time.

Meanwhile, mechanical changes were being made. The Colombo engine's single distributor and inboard plugs were altered with two distributors and plugs repositioned outside the vee. Disc brakes became an

Page opposite, top: An early example of the stylish Ferrari road car, this 250 Europa GT was styled by Giovanni Michelotti and built by his employer, Carrozzeria Vignale. Center: An early-production 250 GT Boano "low-roof" coupe. Bottom: Pinin Farina's original 1956 prototype was little changed when Boano assumed production. This page, top left and right: The restyled 1958 rendition of the PF/Boano coupe was built by the renamed Ellena company and is sometimes referred to as the "high-roof" coupe. Immediate left and below: The second pre-production prototype for the "new-style" Pinin Farina 250 GT coupe as shown in June, 1958. This model replaced the Boano/Ellena as Ferrari's "customer" car. Production lasted through 1962.

Top: A special 250 GT coupe by Pinin Farina circa 1960 with 400 Superamerica-type lines. Above left and right: An unusual example of Zagato coachwork on the 250 GT chassis. Lower right: This Series I 250 GT Cabriolet show car appeared at the 1957 Turin Salon.

optional extra, and were later made standard. The offset shifter on the four-speed transmission gave way to a central shift and electrically operated overdrive.

It would seem that, after a slow beginning, Ferrari wanted to get as many passenger models on the market as quickly as possible, especially now that he had a basic power unit that was not only totally reliable but also capable of ultra-high speeds. It was a classic case of good marketing: a variety of products to meet a variety of customer needs.

As noted, the Boano cabriolet on the Ferrari stand at Geneva '56 was intended for production, but the project was dropped for

some unknown reason. It was thus left to Pinin Farina to carry through with it. The 250 GT cabriolet was not the first open Ferrari, but it would be the first to see regular production. It was first seen in prototype form (chassis no. 0655 GT) at the 1957 Geneva show. (This particular car

was subsequently used by factory driver Peter Collins as his personal transport.) In all, there were four prototypes built before the final production version appeared at the Paris Salon that fall. Only 40 or so of the Series I cars were made. They can be identified by their vertical front

Top: Another one-off Pinin Farina exercise on the versatile 250 GT platform. This one was created in 1958 for Princess Liliane of Belgium. Left: This appears to be a Series I 250 GT cabriolet, built from 1957-59. Grille and headlamp treatments changed during the production run, making it easy to confuse this model with the concurrent long-wheelbase 250 GT Spyder California. Below: Origin of the 250 GT Cabriolet was this Pinin Farina spyder shown in 1957. Curious dipped beltline was thankfully discarded on series cars.

bumperettes and horizontal rear bumpers. Apart from a few early examples, there were no front fender vents and, except for a handful of the final cars, headlamps were covered with perspex. Later models also had horizontal front bumpers. It is doubtful whether any two of these cars were exactly alike since they were more or less built to individual order. There had, once again, been minor changes in the Colombo engine, which in these cabriolets reverted to inboard spark plugs and a single distributor.

Confusing the history of 250 GT cabriolet is a second open model, the flawlessly styled 250 GT California Spyder. It was also penned by Pinin Farina, but body construction was handled by Scaglietti. Both models were built on the long 2600mm (102.4-inch) wheelbase. There was also an even prettier short-wheelbase

California built on the 94.5-inch swb berlinetta chassis. Production was only about 50, running from mid-1960 to early 1963. Pinin Farina also introduced a second 250 GT cabriolet, the Series II, in 1959. This ran concurrently with the Series I for a time, and remained in production until 1962. Some 210 of them were built.

There can be little doubt the commercial success of the Pinin Farina coupe and cabriolet wasn't lost on Enzo Ferrari, and it asked a question. Why not build something for the family man who would appreciate thoroughbred road manners combined with luxury? After all, Aston Martin had come up with the DB4; the Maserati 3500, while not strictly a 2+2, did at least offer some room behind the driver and front passenger. Accordingly, Pinin Farina built a prototype for a four-place coupe (chassis no. 1287 GT). Its clean styling was marked by a row of louvers on the rear sail panels and chrome headlight rims. It was finished in silver, and had a red leather interior. After a full year of testing, Pinin Farina started two more prototypes towards the end of March 1960. One (chassis no. 1895 GT) was used as a "pace car" for that year's Le Mans, which was good publicity as Ferraris finished the 24 Hours 1st, 2nd, 4th, 5th, 6th, and 7th overall. This car was painted *rosso rubino* and had a natural leather interior. Its headlights were slightly recessed in the front fenders and the louvers had disappeared. The third prototype (chassis no. 1903 GT) was white with red leather upholstery. All three had fog lamps placed in the outer ends of a somewhat oval-shaped grille.

The production version, designated 250 GTE 2+2, was shown at Paris and London in

Top and center: The beautiful short-wheelbase 250 GT Spyder California evolved from the earlier lwb model. Car shown has several non-standard fittings. Bottom: The Series II 250 GT cabriolet displays clean Pininfarina lines typical of the early '60s.

Above and left: Ferrari moved into the "family car" market with the 250 GTE 2+2, shown here in its ultimate 1961-62 production form. Basic long-wheelbase 250 chassis was used, but drivetrain was positioned further forward to open up a tiny rear seat area. Below: Another view of the 250 GTE 2+2. The Pininfarina styling is neat and clean, but was criticized in contemporary reports as lacking distinction. Production ran through 1963.

This page: Bearing one of Pinin Farina's most elegantly designed bodies, the 250 GT Berlinetta Lusso was the most luxurious roadgoing Ferrari built up to the early '60s, hence its "luxury" name. Car above was photographed in Scotland. Page opposite: This 1962 show car was Lusso prototype. Note Superfast-style front end with recessed, covered headlamps.

1960. These cars had side fender vents either cut in or applied as panels and no fog lamps. The GTE used the long-wheelbase chassis, and while the car was shorter overall than the 250 GT Pinin Farina coupe it offered more space for passengers and their baggage. To open up room for two small rear seats, the engine/gearbox was moved forward in the chassis. The classic Ferrari grille style was retained but smaller than on the 250 GT coupe. Production continued into 1963, by which time well over 900 had been constructed.

Although this new 2+2 was a good-looking car by any standard, it was and is overshadowed by the 250 GT berlinettas. This is reflected in the wide price

difference between the two models on today's collector market. For example, a good GTE would only fetch around $15,500 whereas a short-wheelbase berlinetta can command $80,000 or more. Nonetheless, the 250 GTE 2+2 was important. It proved that a Ferrari could offer

four-passenger seating and still look and perform like a Ferrari.

When the 250 GTE 2+2 was introduced, the lwb 250 GT coupe was phased out in favor of the steel-bodied 250 GT swb berlinetta. That model continued into the early part of 1963, but its demise was heralded earlier by

the arrival of the GTO. However, there was never any idea that the GTO should have a long production run.

Then at the Paris Salon in October 1962, Ferrari debuted the two-seat 250 GT Berlinetta Lusso. (Lusso means "luxurious" or "luxury," but it was never factory nomenclature.) The powerplant was still the old-faithful Colombo V-12 in its 2953cc (180.2-cid) form, set in the usual sort of chassis with the short 2400mm (94.5-inch) wheelbase. The rear suspension was given the added refinement of concentric "helper" springs around the telescopic shock absorbers and lateral axle location was by Watt linkage, both features borrowed from the GTO. All-disc brakes were standard. Styling, by Pinin Farina, was an amalgam of the swb and GTO designs, resulting in what many consider to be the most handsome of all Ferraris. The body, built by Scaglietti, was made of steel except for the doors, hood, and trunklid, which were aluminum. Unlike all Ferrari road cars up to this time, the Lusso had genuine bucket seats giving considerable lateral support (but unfortunately no backrest rake adjustment or even forward tilt). Outward vision, though, was superb due to the slim roof pillars. Around 350 Lussos were built through 1964. Good specimens still command moderately high prices today but do not cost anywhere near as much as competition Ferraris. The Lusso was last of the under-3.0-liter V-12 road cars, but it was hardly the last of the great front-engine Ferrari GTs.

Aurelio Lampredi had carried out development work on the 60-degree Colombo V-12, but still felt that only large-displacement unsupercharged engines could bring the prestige Ferrari sought in grand prix and sports car racing. Now the Colombo engine had more than its share of race victories, but in supercharged form it gulped too much fuel. This meant pit stops were usually necessary to finish races that the unsupercharged cars could complete without refueling. Colombo did not agree with Lampredi in this, and left Ferrari to return to Alfa Romeo, which favored supercharging for its GP cars. The Lampredi engines in their various configurations were very successful in competition, but it should not be forgotten that the Colombo was still capable of winning even in the early '70s.

Lampredi's first try at a sports/racing car was the 275S. It would be a test bed for a 4.5-liter (274.6-cid) unsupercharged engine intended for grand prix use, this being the maximum displacement for Formula 1 at the time. Two cars powered by a 3322cc/202.7-cid (bore and stroke 72 x 68mm/2.83 x 2.68 inches) V-12 were driven in the 1950 Mille Miglia by Alberto Ascari and Luigi Villoresi, but they were troubled by tire problems and retired with transmission failure. Engine output was alleged to be 270 bhp at 7000 rpm, but this figure probably related to the F1 prototype while the actual 275S would have had a more modest 230 bhp.

The next development was the 340 America, Ferrari's first big sports car. It was announced in late summer 1950, and a brochure issued in October gave engine displacement as 4101cc/250.3 cid (80 x 68mm/3.15 x 2.68 inches). With three Weber 40 DCF twin-choke carburetors and a compression ratio of 8:1, the 340 engine delivered a maximum 220

THE FRONT V~12 SPORTS/RACING CARS OVER 3.0 LITERS

bhp at 6000 rpm. The Paris Salon in October saw the first complete car, a black barchetta by Touring. It looked very much like the 212 Export barchetta, but had a slightly longer 2420mm (95.3-inch) wheelbase. Its first racing win came at the 1951 Mille Miglia, with Villoresi and Cassini driving. However, it won only once more that year in Europe, taking the Portuguese Grand Prix. A number of the 340 Americas went *to* America, where they were campaigned by Bill Spear, Henry Manney, Jim Kimberly, Jack McAfee, and others. There were probably about 25 built. Some had barchetta and berlinetta bodies by Touring, others were Vignale-bodied coupes and spyders.

The 340 America was soon joined by the 340 Mille Miglia and 340 Mexico. But at the Brussels show, Ferrari had another surprise: a chassis for a new *gran turismo* to be called the 342 America. A complete car was on view at Turin a few months later, but for some reason Ferrari severely limited production of this

model; no more than six or so were built.

All the 340 had a five-speed non-synchromesh gearbox in unit with the engine. Each series had a different wheelbase length; the 340 America had 2420mm (95.3 inches), the 340 MM 2500mm (98.4), and the 340 Mexico 2600mm (102.3 inches). Early

Above: A Ghia-bodied 340 America coupe is readied for the 1952 Carrera Panamericana. Jack McAfee drove it. Below: Pinin Farina's beautiful 375 Mille Miglia spyder from 1954.

340s had three two-choke Weber carburetors. By 1953, the MMs were using three four-choke Webers, boosting output to a rated 300 bhp. The America was rated at 220 bhp, the Mexico at 280 bhp.

This page: One of three of the 340 Mexico berlinettas built for the 1952 Carrera Panamericana. Despite its sleek road-car appearance, this model was admirably well-suited for the rigors of the dusty long-distance Mexican race. Page opposite: A rare 375 Mille Miglia spyder. This 1954 example has never been raced, but instead was modified for street use from new. Pinin Farina penned the smooth sports/racing body marked by a detachable metal tonneau on the passenger's side and a long hood to house the big 4.9-liter V-12.

Four 340 Mexicos were built in 1952 for the Carrera Panamericana. Three had berlinetta bodies. The fourth was a spyder (for Bill Spear) that never started the race, though it was later campaigned successfully in the States. It was Bracco, however, who won with the 250 MM berlinetta. The next big win for the 340 didn't come until 1953, when Villoresi won the Tour of Sicily in April with an MM. Similar cars took 1st, 4th, and 9th places at the Mille Miglia; drivers were Marzotto, American Tom Cole, and Giulio Cabianca, respectively. The last factory outing for the MM was that year's Le Mans, where Gianni and Marzotto finished 5th in a berlinetta. Most of those cars found their way to the United States where they were raced for a time. Although certainly faster than competitors like the Mercedes 300SL, the Jaguar C-Type and the new V-6 Lancias, the 340 series could not be considered one of the more

successful sports/racing Ferraris. Nevertheless, Ferrari and his engineers were still experimenting, and their cars clearly needed something besides sheer power.

Le Mans 1953 also saw the first appearance of the new 4.5-liter sports/racing car, designated 375 MM. In the capable hands of

Ascari and Villoresi it set the race lap record, but retired with clutch problems. Its 4494cc/274.2-cid engine (80 x 74.5 mm/3.15 x 2.93 inches) was the one that had been developed for the 1952 Indianapolis 500. There were two versions of this car, the factory's racer and a customer model with a capacity of 4522cc (275.8 cid).

Open and closed bodies were offered, all by Pinin Farina. As with many early Ferraris it's difficult to be precise about 375 MM production; it could have been between a dozen and 18.

For 1954 the factory 375s were boosted to 4.9 liters (299 cid) by combining the 84mm (3.30-inch) bore of the customer 375 MM with

This page, above: Umberto Maglioli in the 375 Plus on the way to victory in the 1954 Mexican Road Race. Right: The competition 375 MM berlinetta as shown at Brussels in January, 1954. There was also a road version. Both were styled by Pinin Farina. Page opposite: The 375 Plus had a limited racing career and limited production: only six were built, two with faired-in headrests.

the 74.5mm (2.93-inch) stroke of the factory car. Six of these cars, named 375 Plus, were made. They featured a new chassis that differed in many respects from those on previous Ferrari sports/racers. Two of its major highlights were frame rails that ran up and over the back axle and use of a rear transaxle with de Dion tube as on some of Ferrari's grand prix cars. The spyder bodies were made by Pinin Farina, and two of the cars had faired-in headrests. While this model competed only briefly it certainly made its presence felt. On its first outing it won at Agadir in the hands of Giuseppe Farina, followed by a win at Silverstone with Foilan Gonzales at the wheel. Gonzales and Maurice Trintignant then scored at Le Mans. In November, Umberto

Maglioli was the victor in the tough 1954 Carrera Panamericana. The 375 MM was still winning, too. Masten Gregory captured two important 1954 events, and Phil Hill and co-driver Richie Ginther were right behind Maglioli in the Mexico race.

The 375 Plus was powerful, brutish-looking, and all muscle. It was said that when one went by you could not only hear it but feel it! All six cars were sold at the end of the season. Most, if not all, were bought by Americans, who

raced them for several more years. (In those days, even rare Ferrari models were bought to be driven and driven hard, like all Ferraris should be, and not simply as investments.) Three of these cars survive today: one in France, one in South America, and the third in Australia. Two were crashed, one in the 1954 Mexico event, the other in the 1954 Mille Miglia. Whereabouts of the sixth car are unknown, but it's probably in the States, though likely without an engine.

Ferrari was never one to

remain idle, and during the next few years he issued number of experimental models built in tiny numbers. One was the 410 Sport, an interim type with a displacement of 4962cc (302.8 cid). Its engine was familiar Ferrari: single camshaft per cylinder bank, two plugs per cylinder, and three Weber (42 DCZ4) carburetors. Like the 375 Plus, the 410 Sport had its gearbox in unit with the differential, although it had a five-speed instead of a four-speed. Four cars were built, but only two

were actually raced (in the 1956 Buenos Aires 1000 km). They were meant for the 1955 Carrera Panamericana, but that race was cancelled, like a number of others that year, in the wake of the horrifying accident at Le Mans. These cars had the suffix CM on their chassis numbers, which indicates they had been built especially for the Mexican Road Race (Carrera Mexico). They were sold after their outing in Argentina.

The 1955 season had been an unsatisfactory one for Ferrari.

The 1954 campaign had seen the decline of his four-cylinder grand prix cars (625, Squalo, and Supersqualo), and he now lacked a new design for Formula 1. On top of all that, the Le Mans disaster had panicked the FIA into cancelling the French, German, Swiss, and Spanish grands prix fearing that the various governments might ban auto racing outright unless better spectator safety measures could be implemented. Enzo possibly blamed some of the '55 season's troubles on Lampredi. Although

Above: The brutish 410 Sport was intended for the 1955 Mexican Road Race, which was cancelled. Only four of this interim type were built, and only two actually raced.

he had produced some great cars over five years, Lampredi had become disenchanted with the Ferrari organization, and left for Fiat before year's end. With him ended the reign of the large-displacement front-engine sports/racing formula at Ferrari.

But there was one piece of good news in 1955. The Lancia D50 grand prix cars and their equipment were handed over to Ferrari by order of the Italian government after Lancia went technically bankrupt. Vittorio Jano, who had worked with Ferrari in the '20s and '30s, came with the deal, as did Alberto Massimino.

For 1956 there was an entirely new racing engine created by the Ferrari design team now headed by Jano. It combined the best of both the Colombo and Lampredi V-12s. Bore and stroke were 73 x 69.5mm (2.87 x 2.74 inches) for 3490cc (212.9 cid). Three Weber 40 DCF carburetors and a 9.1:1 compression ratio were specified for a power output of 320 bhp at

7300 rpm. The engine was slotted into a new model, the 290 Mille Miglia. It wasn't ready for either Buenos Aires or Sebring, but two cars made it to the Tour of Sicily in April. Castelloti set the pace but retired with transmission

failure, while Musso's car misfired from the start. Peter Collins won the race in a four-cylinder 860 Monza, although he drove for most of the 10 hours without a clutch. The 290 MM made a better showing in the 23rd Mille Miglia at the end of April. Weather was appalling, with heavy rainstorms and near zero visibility at times. Despite this, the Ferrari steamroller ran on to take the first five places. Castelotti was 1st in the 290 MM, followed by Collins and Musso in 860 Monzas, Juan Manuel Fangio 4th in a 290 MM, and Gendebien 5th in a new lightweight 250 GT berlinetta.

A single 290 MM was entered for the 1956 Targa Florio, but it was wrecked in practice when Hans Herrmann found himself upside down in a deep ditch after swerving to avoid a truck. The next championship race, the Nurburgring, saw the Musso/Trintignant cars crash while the second 290 MM, driven during the race by no less than four team members, placed 3rd behind an 860 Monza. The final event was held on the Kristianstad circuit, the 1000km

Sports Car GP of Sweden. Three 290 MMs and two 860 Monzas were entered. In a curious incident, Robert Manzon, driving the Peter Collins 290 MM, broke an oil line, and the spillage sent him off the track into a nearby wheatfield. Collins and Phil Hill also found the oil and went into the wheat, but managed to get back on course. There was a great deal of driver switching during the race, but eventually Hill and Trintignant brought the V-12 home in 1st place. Ferrari took five of the first six places—and the Sports Car Championsip for the third time.

The 290 MM got a new cylinder head for 1957, with twin overhead camshafts for each bank. Three of the quad-cam cars and one twin-cam car were sent to Buenos Aires for the season opener, but two retired with low oil pressure and ignition problems. The twin-cam car won, averaging over 100 mph, and the remaining four-cam entry came in 4th. These quad-cam cars were designated 290 Sports, but after this race their engines were reworked to 3783cc (230.8 cid) and the designation changed to 315 Sport. At Sebring the best they could do was 6th and 7th, thus ending this model's short life. Ferrari had three new cars prepared for the Mille Miglia. These used a modified 315 Sport power unit bored out to 77mm (3.03 inches) and stroked to 72mm (2.83 inches)

A young Phil Hill poses with the 3.5-liter 290 MM sports/racer (left). Hill shared driving chores in this car (above) with Masten Gregory (below) at the 1956 Sebring 12 Hours. The Ferrari proved competitive but trouble-prone, and retired after only four hours because of a burned out main bearing.

for 4023cc (245.5 cid). This model was designated 335 Sport. All of this can leave the uninitiated quite bewildered. De Portago shared one of the 335s with Ed Nelson. Running in 4th some 25 miles from the finish, he crashed, killing himself, his co-driver, and 10 spectators. Because of this accident two of the Ferraris were impounded for inspection, leaving only one 335 for the Nurburgring 1000 km, where it placed 2nd (Collins/Gendebien). In retrospect, this four-cam engine was not a success, scoring only two victories that season.

Ferrari fielded another sports/racing car for 1957. First seen at Silverstone, it was the 296S with a 300-bhp V-6. For the grand prix at Spa in May, which was open to unlimited-capacity sports cars, a new engine was used. This was derived from the 290 Sport unit, but with stroke reduced from 69.5mm to 58.8mm (2.74 to 2.31), the same as the 250 MM and 250 GT. Sometimes referred to as a "Super Testa Rossa" this car was designated 312 S or 312 LM. With six two-throat Weber 38 DCN carburetors and a 9.5:1 compression ratio, the revised V-6 was rated at 320 bhp at 8200 rpm. It was reportedly capable of up to 9500 rpm, but had little power below the 6000 mark. The chassis had a new four-speed transaxle and transverse shaft mounted on the left of the final drive. The rear suspension was De Dion with a transverse leaf spring. Proposed as a prototype for 1959, it was driven at the '58 Spa GP by Gendebien, but gearbox problems put it out of contention. It is thought that this chassis with a 335S engine (possibly from De Portago's crashed 1957 Mille Miglia car) was used for the June 1958 "Race of Two Worlds" at Monza.

The story behind this race is an interesting historical footnote. In 1956, the Automobile Club of Italy had announced it would stage a 500-mile race the following year on the new high-speed banked track at Monza. The leading Indy cars from America would be invited to compete with the best from Europe. Some greeted the idea with enthusiasm, others were more skeptical. Some European press writers stated that in their opinion, the chassis design of the American cars was antiquated. They also derided the widespread use of proprietary components such as gearboxes, wheels, and brakes. Both these observations were true enough, but the U.S. cars varied a great deal in mechanical detail, and they were far superior in construction to most contemporary European grand prix and sports/racing cars. (Many GP competitors have since taken a leaf from the American racing book in making mainly 'kit' cars; only constructors such as Ferrari, Renault, and Alfa Romeo manufacture most — though not all — of the components used in their Formula 1 machines.)

The European constructors made a half-hearted effort, and the new drivers' trade union, the UPPI, boycotted the race as being too dangerous. However, the race went ahead, and the fans were treated to some spectacular high-speed driving not usually seen in Europe. Victory went to the Indy racers, but Jaguars took 4th, 5th, and 6th places after a number of the U.S. cars suffered breakdowns on the bumpy Monza circuit. The Indy drivers gladly agreed to a return match scheduled the following year.

Formula 1 pilots also decided to enter the 1958 race. One reason no doubt was the sizable prize money offered. Ferrari wasn't too keen on the idea, but the Italian Automobile Club persuaded him to participate in the second Race

of Two Worlds. It wasn't long before two cars were being prepared at Maranello.

It was decided to use the 4023cc (245.5-cid) 335S V-12, which was now superfluous for sports/racing as the displacement limit for 1958 had been lowered to 3.0 liters. Five of these engines were available plus chassis, and Ferrari felt that if this car could acquit itself in the event he might be able to sell copies in the States. The chassis was similar in many respects to that of the Gendebien car at Spa 1957, but it was strengthened to withstand the Monza track's bumpy surface, and a three-speed gearbox was installed. The body was similar to that of the 1958 Dino 246

Created for the 1958 "Race of Two Worlds" at Monza, the 412 MI was a unique Ferrari hybrid, combining the 250 Testa Rossa chassis with the 4.1-liter four-cam V-12 from the 335 S. The car was later acquired by California Ferrari distributor John von Neumann, and was seen occasionally in historic auto races through the early '70s (the photo far left shows the car competing in one such race at Pebble Beach). Bodywork was altered after the car ran at Monza in 1958 from single-seat to this two-seat form.

Formula 1 car, but was more bulbous and had an ugly narrow tail. This new large-capacity racer was dubbed the 412 MI (Monza/Indianapolis).

To back up the MI the factory also sent a standard F1 Dino 246 with a 2962cc (180.6-cid) V-6, a car Mike Hawthorn had driven at Silverstone in May. Chassis alterations consisted of an experimental De Dion coil spring system at the rear and use of twin Houdaille shock absorbers at each corner, again because of the rough racing surface. The body was similar in appearance to the Dino F1 except for a short stubby tail and a high perspex screen. This car was designated 296 MI. Both entries were shod with Firestone racing tires (Ferrari was contracted to use Belgian Englebert tires, but they tended to throw treads at Monza).

A third Ferrari was entered by Luigi Chinetti's North American Racing Team (NART) for Harry Schell. This car was a Type 375 variant, reputedly built for the 1953 Indianapolis 500 (Mike Hawthorn believed it was the car driven by Villoresi at Silverstone and Boreham in 1952). For the Monza 500 its 4.5-liter (274.6-cid) engine was reduced to 4.2 liters (256.3 cid) to conform with displacement regs. Similar in appearance to the old 375 F1 except for a bulbous tank and a high curved windshield, it was painted in U.S. racing colors, blue and white.

Hawthorn found the handling of the 412 MI atrocious on the concrete bankings. Despite this, he reeled off several laps in practice at 165 mph. Juan Manuel Fangio put in three consecutive laps at 171.5 mph. (Grid positions were determined by the highest average speed over that distance.) Then, Luigi Musso recorded 174.67 mph, and took pole position for the first heat.

The '58 Race of Two Worlds was run in three heats over 63 laps, with 90 minutes in between. In the first, Musso led the pack for six laps after the rolling start. Sachs then took the lead, and for the next 15 laps two American

cars and Musso took turns pacing the field. On lap 20, Sachs' engine cried enough. Six laps later, Musso, overcome by methanol fumes and the effort of driving a real handful of a car, had to be relieved by Hawthorn after all four wheels were changed (the rear spokes were breaking up and the tires badly scrubbed). Hawthorn finished 6th, with the American cars taking the first three places. The NART entry driven by Schell came in 12th out of 15 finishers. Phil Hill had to retire the 296 MI because of distributor trouble. The second heat was won by American Jim Rathman, making it two in a row for the U.S. The 412 MI driven by Musso and Hill could manage only 9th. The NART car was now out of it due to a number of problems. Rathman then took the third heat, beating Jimmy Bryan by 26.7 seconds, and Hill brought the Ferrari home 3rd, three laps behind the winners. The Race of Two Worlds was never run again.

In 1958, John von Neumann, the Ferrari distributor for California, was looking for a "hot" car to compete against American-built specials in SCCA and California sports car events.

The 412 MI engine was duly installed in a 1958 Testa Rossa chassis and delivered to von Neumann. Two Marelli distributors fired two spark plugs per cylinder. With six Weber 42 DCH/3 carburetors and a 9.9:1 compression ratio, horsepower was rated at 440 at 8000 rpm. Unfortunately, the car did not perform as well as it might have, even in the hands of pros like Hill and Ginther. It went through a number of owners, including the late Bill Harrah.

For 1962, the previous World Sports Car Championship was replaced by a championship for GT cars. At the same time, sports/racing cars up to 3.0 liters and experimental or prototype GT cars up to 4.0 liters were allowed to run together at long-distance events like Le Mans and Sebring. Ferrari's plans for 1962 included cars for the 3.0-liter class only; he was notified about the 4.0-liter prototype class too late, and doing well in it wasn't of any particular commercial value to him. This reasoning seemed a little strange because, at the time, the 4.0-liter Type 400 Superamerica was being built in small numbers, and these cars were much more salable in

the American market than the 3.0-liter models. Enzo must have had a change of heart, for at the April Le Mans trials an experimental 4.0-liter car appeared. It had open bodywork similar to that of the Scuderia di Venezia Testa Rossa that had won the Sebring 12-hour race earlier in the year. This car seems to have been designated the 330 TR1/LM or 330 TR1/62, and differed from the Sebring car in one striking way: a full-width horizontal airfoil mounted on vertical struts at approximately windshield height. It was suggested that the power unit was a 400 Superamerica engine modified to Testa Rossa design. Hill and Gendebein drove the car to an overall win at Le Mans, covering 2765.73 miles at an average speed of 115.25 mph.

At his December 1962 press conference, Enzo Ferrari had little to say about his plans for 1963, and there was no new car on show. But the following March he held a second meeting where he introduced two new competition models, the 3.0-liter mid-engine 250 P prototype and a front-engine 4.0-liter V-12 prototype coupe called the 330 LM, which was subsequently renamed 330 LMB (Le Mans Berlinetta). It was both handsome and purposeful-looking, combining the 250 GTO front with the main structure of the 250 GT Berlinetta Lusso. The LMB's hood had neither bulge nor scoop, but the GTO's three air intakes were retained on the nose, and the front fenders had three vertical outlets. The greenhouse was unmistakably Lusso, and there were flap-type "tunnels" over the rear wheel arches for tire clearance. Air outlets were cut in the rear fenders behind the wheel arches. At 2500mm (98.4 inches) the LMB's wheelbase was 100mm (3.93 inches) longer than either the GTO's or Lusso's. Its engine was based on the 400 Superamerica unit, with a single camshaft per bank, one spark plug per cylinder, and bore and stroke of 77 x 71mm (3.03 x 2.79 inches) giving a displacement of 3967cc (242.1 cid). Six 42 DCN twin-choke Webers fed the fuel. Output was rated at 400 bhp at 7500mm.

Mike Parkes and Lorenzo Bandini drove the LMB at Sebring 1963, where it went off course on several occasions due to either poor handling or faulty brakes. On lap 72 it retired after hitting a tree, which caused the fuel tank to split. Three cars appeared at Le Mans (along with a 250 LM entered by NART for Masten Gregory and David Piper, who ended up 6th). Two went out with assorted complaints, but the third one, driven by Jack Sears and Mike Salmon, finished 5th. No further development work was carried out on the LMB; Ferrari was now turning to mid-engine designs.

It should be mentioned that although the later 275 GTB and 365 GTB/4 Daytona were both front-engine V-12s and quite adaptable for GT endurance racing, neither competed under the official factory flag. Instead, they were entered in a variety of races, including Le Mans, by independents engaged by official Ferrari distributors, though the factory usually provided technical assistance.

Page opposite: The 330 LMB was one of the last front-engine competition Ferraris. Styling combined GTO and Berlinetta Lusso elements. This page: The 412 MI in its later two-seat form as driven by Phil Hill and Ritchie Ginther in U.S. events.

At the January 1951 Brussels show Ferrari announced a new model, the 342 America. A completed car appeared at Turin a few months later featuring high-roof coupe coachwork by Touring and the 340 America engine. Wheelbase was 2650mm (104.3 inches) against the 340's 2420mm (95.3-inch) span. As noted previously, production was limited to around a half dozen. Chassis numbers had the suffix AL. Ferrari's next big-engine GT was the 375 America, introduced at the 1953 Paris show with a capacity of 4523cc (276.0 cid). It shared basic chassis design with the Lampredi-engine 250 Europa also on display, but carried a Pininfarina coupe body. Production was again very limited, estimated at no more than 12 (only 9 have been located to date). Chassis numbers for this small series also had the AL suffix.

The 410 Superamerica was a replacement for the 375 America, and was powered by the last of the "true" long-block V-12s. The new model's rolling chassis was displayed first, at the 1955 Paris Salon, the car itself at Brussels 1956. The Superamerica was a very scarce item, with production restricted to perhaps no more than one a month. Coachwork was usually by Pininfarina, but Boano, Ghia, and Scaglietti also designed bodies for this chassis. The first SA had a body similar to but larger than that of the special Pininfarina coupes on the 250 GT chassis. Initially, the SA was built on the long-wheelbase (2800mm/110.2-inch) platform but in 1957 a shorter-wheelbase

THE V~12 GRAN TURISMOS OVER 3.0 LITERS

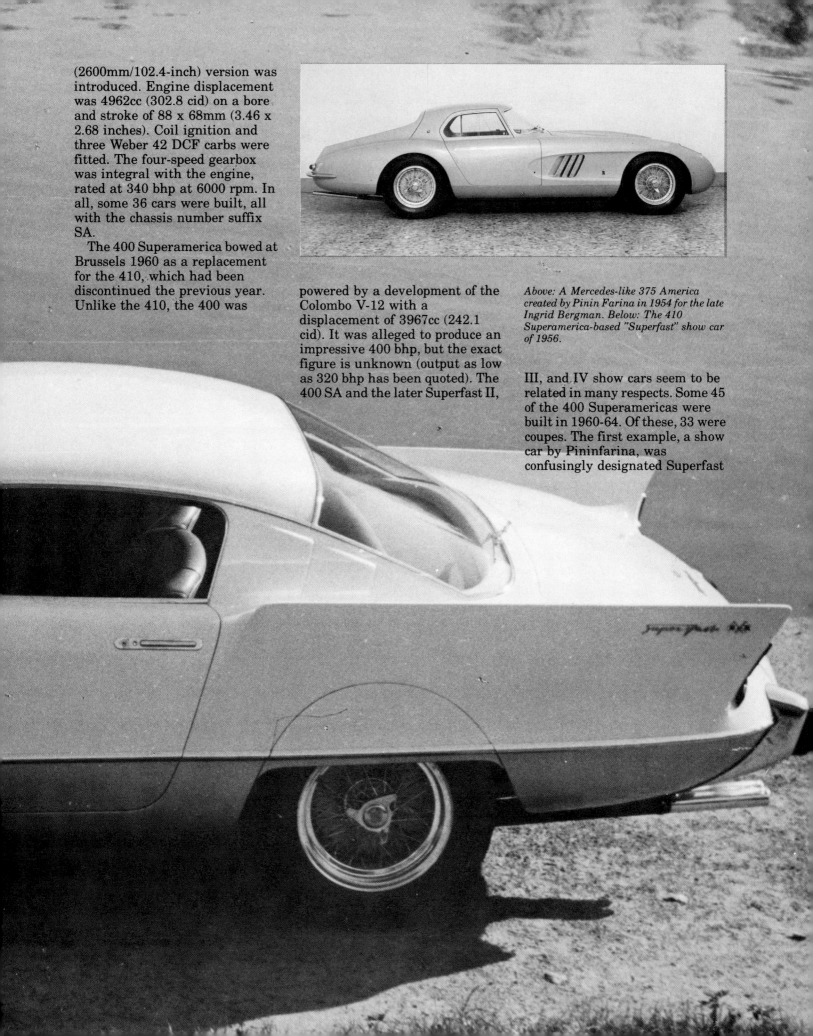

(2600mm/102.4-inch) version was introduced. Engine displacement was 4962cc (302.8 cid) on a bore and stroke of 88 x 68mm (3.46 x 2.68 inches). Coil ignition and three Weber 42 DCF carbs were fitted. The four-speed gearbox was integral with the engine, rated at 340 bhp at 6000 rpm. In all, some 36 cars were built, all with the chassis number suffix SA.

The 400 Superamerica bowed at Brussels 1960 as a replacement for the 410, which had been discontinued the previous year. Unlike the 410, the 400 was powered by a development of the Colombo V-12 with a displacement of 3967cc (242.1 cid). It was alleged to produce an impressive 400 bhp, but the exact figure is unknown (output as low as 320 bhp has been quoted). The 400 SA and the later Superfast II,

Above: A Mercedes-like 375 America created by Pinin Farina in 1954 for the late Ingrid Bergman. Below: The 410 Superamerica-based "Superfast" show car of 1956.

III, and IV show cars seem to be related in many respects. Some 45 of the 400 Superamericas were built in 1960-64. Of these, 33 were coupes. The first example, a show car by Pininfarina, was confusingly designated Superfast

375 America cabriolet by Vignale

375 America cabriolet by Vignale

375 America cabriolet by Pinin Farina, 1958

Special 410 Superamerica coupe by Pinin Farina, 1958

410 Superamerica coupe by Pinin Farina

410 Superamerica coupe by Pinin Farina

410 Superamerica coupe by Pinin Farina, 1957

400 Superamerica "Aerodinamico" by Pinin Farina

410 Superamerica coupe by Pinin Farina

410 Superamerica coupe by Pinin Farina

continued on page 113

410 Superamerica

More distinctive styling for the 410 Superamerica chassis, this time by Pinin Farina, who eschewed fins. Some 12 of these cars were built.

**250 GT Berlinetta
Tour de France**

A much sought-after Ferrari is the long-wheelbase 250 GT Berlinetta, generally known as the Tour de France after the annual race-and-rally event round France which this model won on a number of occasions. The car shown here has been restored for pop singer Eric Clapton, and is looked after by Modena Engineering, the Ferrari distributor in the UK.

250 GT
Spyder California

There were two versions of the 250 GT Spyder California. The long-wheelbase models were in production from late 1957 to early 1960. The short-wheelbase cars took over in 1960 and were built through 1963. As the pictures here show, a Ferrari's engine compartment and cockpit are as handsome in their way as the body.

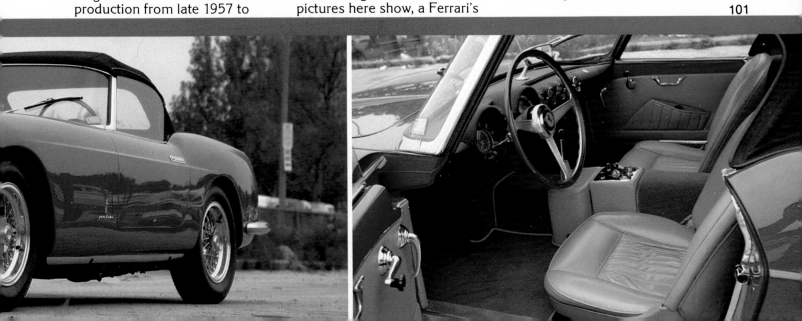

250 GT
Berlinetta Lusso

The 250 GT Berlinetta Lusso (for "luxury") was the first road-going Ferrari that catered to passenger comforts. Similar in many respects to the 250 short-wheelbase models, it also qualifies as a "classic" Ferrari because of its timeless styling. Surprisingly, it does not command the high prices such cars often do. Around 400 were built altogether.

250 GT
Spyder California

Some 46 examples of the 250 GT Spyder California shown here were built. The factory did not officially use either the GT or Spyder designations, however. The idea for this model was suggested by Ferrari's U.S. distributor. As in so many other cases, Pininfarina styled the body, which was constructed by Scaglietti.

250 GT swb
Berlinetta

Perhaps one of the best-known Ferraris—certainly one of the most sought-after. It won many races in the hands of factory drivers and independents alike, and is the epitome of the dual-purpose sports machine. It's the 250 GT short-wheelbase berlinetta, introduced in 1959.

250 GT swb
Berlinetta

Adrian Conan Doyle, son of Sherlock Holmes' creator, was the early owner of this 250 GT short-wheelbase berlinetta, which now belongs to ardent UK Ferrarist Bill Lake. Note the differences in nose treatment between this car and another example of the same type shown on the previous page.

Type 196SP
& Dino 196S

Above: The 196SP was a mid-engine sports/racing car, and only one was built as such. Two others appeared in the following year, 1963, but these were reworks of other models. Below: The Dino 196S, a front-engine sports/racing machine built in 1959. It's extremely rare: only two known examples were built.

250 GTO

Perhaps the most glamorous of Ferraris, the 250 GTO had a distinguished racing career. A good one can fetch $150,000 and up on today's market.

II, and is quite well known. Of the remaining 12, perhaps 10 were cabriolets and the other two bodied to customer order.

The Superfast cars, except for the production 500 series, were all one-of-a-kind styling and engineering exercises built for auto show duty and other special requirements. "Superfast I" was shown at the 1956 Paris Salon. Styled by Pinin Farina, it was a short-wheelbase (2600mm/102.4-inch) coupe on the 410 Superamerica chassis and fitted with the wet-sump version of the 4.9-liter engine from the 410 Sport. Body design featured a cantilever roof without windshield pillars. In the American idiom of the mid-'50s, prominent tailfins and a wide low grille were its main styling features. The 4.9 Superfast followed at the 1957 Turin show. It was another Pinin Farina coupe with lines similar to those of the first Superfast but without its fins or cantilever roof. Next, Farina designed and built Superfast II for the 1960 Turin show. Called an "aerodinamica" coupe, this was believed to be Farina's personal car at one time. Again, the short-wheelbase 410 Superamerica chassis was used for this very attractive car, marked by a small grille and retractable headlights. Another version was seen at Turin the following year with an enlarged grille and a hood scoop, but without the earlier car's rear wheel skirts. The 400 SA chassis formed the basis for Superfast III, which appeared at Geneva in 1962 and was obviously derived from Superfast II. The hood scoop was retained, but for some reason a retractable cover was provided for the grille and rear wheels were partially enclosed. Superfast IV also appeared in 1962, again on the 400 Superamerica chassis. Similar in most ways to the two previous models, it differed in having exposed quad headlamps

Top and center: The first Superfast show car as seen at Paris 1956. The chassis came from the 410 Superamerica. Bottom: The unique Superfast III from Geneva 1962.

and open rear wheel arches.

The only Superfast produced in volume — if 37 cars can be considered volume — was the 500. First shown at the 1964 Geneva Salon, it remained in the Ferrari catalog through 1966. Body design was, as usual, by Pininfarina, and was a natural evolution of the 410/400 Superamerica. The 4963cc (302.9-cid) displacement was new, but the engine showed Colombo's influence. Some features and components were borrowed from the big 330 GT 2+2, such as the four-speed overdrive gearbox on early models (changed to a five-speed later adopted for the 330). The 500 Superfast was a handsome car of very masculine character, and lived up to its name on the straightaways.

After a long run of 250 GTs, Ferrari introduced the 330 GT 2+2 at the 1963 Paris Salon. Coachwork was initially as for the 250 GTE, but because of the 3967cc (242.1-cid) engine, the type designation 330 America was used as an interim measure. About 50 of these cars were marketed towards the end of the year. The first proper 330 GT had revised styling marked by a four-headlamp front. It was shown at Brussels early in 1964. The engine was based on the Colombo design, and boasted 300 bhp at 6600 rpm. Chassis layout was similar to the 250 GT's. As noted previously, a four-speed-plus-overdrive gearbox was used, with a five-speed installed on later cars. Many critics suggested this model was too ordinary and lacked the style expected of a Ferrari. Nevertheless, it was spacious for a 2+2 with plenty of headroom for rear-seat passengers, and it was no sluggard. After 625 examples, a Mark II version appeared in 1965. This reverted to two headlamps, and had reshaped rear fenders and front fender vents. Some 455 were built through 1968, bringing total series production to 1080, quite sizable for a single Ferrari model.

One of the most handsome and exciting designs from the pen of

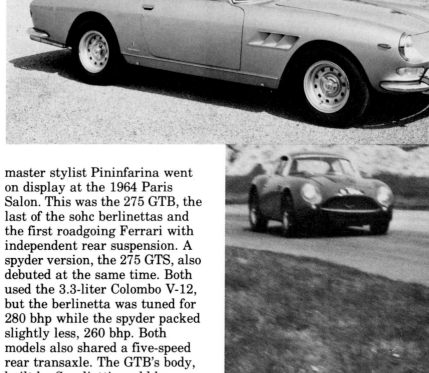

master stylist Pininfarina went on display at the 1964 Paris Salon. This was the 275 GTB, the last of the sohc berlinettas and the first roadgoing Ferrari with independent rear suspension. A spyder version, the 275 GTS, also debuted at the same time. Both used the 3.3-liter Colombo V-12, but the berlinetta was tuned for 280 bhp while the spyder packed slightly less, 260 bhp. Both models also shared a five-speed rear transaxle. The GTB's body, built by Scaglietti, could be ordered in steel with aluminum panels or with all-aluminum construction. The GTS body was designed and built by Pininfarina with lines evolved from the 330 GT 2+2. Although functional, the spyder lacked the styling panache of the berlinetta. The GTB could be ordered with six Weber 40 DCZ/6 carburetors instead of the

standard triple Weber 40 DCZ/6 or 40 DF1/1 carbs. Campagnolo alloy wheels were standard (the first Ferrari not to have standard wire wheels) with Borrani wire wheels available at extra cost. The GTS came only with three

carbs and the wire wheels; there were no options.

A second-series GTB appeared at Frankfurt 1965. Minor styling changes comprised a hood bulge to clear the carburetors, a driver's door without the vent wing previously fitted, and external hinges for the trunklid to provide a bit more luggage room. A month later at Paris, the car's nose had been lengthened and the grille made slightly smaller. By the time of the Brussels show in January 1966, revised alloy wheels had been fitted, and the driveshaft was encased in a torque tube, an idea also tried on the 330 GTC.

Ferrari also built a few (11 in all) competition coupes designated 275 GTB/C. All these had special camshafts, valves, pistons, crankshaft, and carburetors, and employed dry-sump lubrication.

Two years after the GTB's introduction, a much revised model was shown at Paris 1966.

Above left and right: The 275 GTB/4 appeared in 1966. Styling was modified a bit from the original design and a new four-cam cylinder head was added making this the first quad-cam Ferrari road car. Right: Only 11 of the competition 275 GTB/C berlinettas were constructed.

Although outwardly similar in appearance, this 275 GTB/4 had a four-cam V-12 with 300 bhp at 8000 rpm under its hood. It was the first roadgoing Ferrari with twin cams on each cylinder bank, hence the type designation. As with the later 275s, power was transmitted to the five-speed transaxle via a torque tube. In 1967, a special cabriolet version was built at the request of Luigi Chinetti Jr., son of the American Ferrari distributor. Constructed by Scaglietti from a basic GTB bodyshell, it was called the NART Spyder (for Chinetti's North American Racing Team). Only 9 copies were built, making this a very exclusive, very desirable commodity.

From any angle the 275 GTB design is one of the world's most stunning pieces of automotive sculpture. It still turns heads everywhere, yet it has a timeless quality that stands as a tribute to Pininfarina's artistry. In all, around 350 of the beautiful GTB/4s were produced—each able to see 155 mph or better. Some 450 of the first-series GTBs were constructed. GTS production totalled 200.

The *gran turismo* Ferraris had been undergoing a subtle change which had really begun with the 250 GT Berlinetta Lusso. Comfort and refinement were being given increasing emphasis. The early concept of the GT as a thinly veiled racing car had all but disappeared.

A very civilized and, in the opinion of many, the best Ferrari road car yet bowed at Geneva in March 1966. The new 330 GTC utilized the 275 GTB chassis and the 3967cc (242.1-cid) engine from the 330 GT 2+2. Pininfarina combined the 400 Superamerica front styling and the 275 GTS rear end to create a most elegant and handsome automobile. Although the GTC had the same displacement as the 330 GT 2+2 its block was new, designed to accept a rear transaxle, which required different engine and differential mountings. Suspension was, of course, all-independent, and disc brakes were used at each wheel. About 600 of these cars were constructed through 1968. The GTC was not only civilized, it was also quiet. In fact, it was probably the first Ferrari in which you could actually enjoy a radio. Air conditioning was offered as an option, again reflecting the increasing refinement of the GTs. A convertible model, the 330 GTS, was introduced at Paris in 1966. It had the same specifications as the coupe, and was phased out at the same time. However, both models continued through 1970 as the 365 GTC and GTS with the 4.4-liter engine from the 365 GT 2+2. Appearance and specifications were otherwise unchanged.

Left top, center, and below: The 330 GTC introduced in 1966 was the most civilized two-seat Ferrari road car yet. An engine change in 1968 changed designation to 365 GTC. Above: The 275 GTS was given a different front end to become the 330 GTS. Bottom: The brawny 365 California Spyder was another new arrival for 1966.

In the meantime, the 365 California convertible had been introduced at Geneva in the spring of 1966 as a luxury car in the mold of the 410/400 Superamericas and 500 Superfast. It, too, carried the 4.4-liter V-12 and a five-speed gearbox. Its production run lasted only into 1967, and only about 14 were produced.

The largest, heaviest Ferrari road car yet seen premiered at the 1967 Paris Salon, the 365 GT 2+2. Again, power was supplied by the 4.4-liter V-12, but with the gearbox mounted directly behind. This was the first Ferrari 2+2 with all-independent suspension, which employed Koni shock absorbers and concentric coil springs at each wheel. Power steering and air conditioning were standard, as was a self-leveling rear suspension developed jointly by Koni and Ferrari. Wheelbase was 2650mm (104.3 inches) as on the 330 2+2, but styling was more closely related to the 500 Superfast, especially at the front, than other recent 2+2 designs. *Road & Track* magazine called it Ferrari's first "sedan," which indicates just how plush and sophisticated Ferrari road cars had become by the late '60s.

The next model among the over-3.0-liter Ferrari GTs became a legend in its own time, and is one of the most sought-after cars today, bar none. The 365 GTB/4, dubbed Daytona by the press, was introduced in October 1968 at the Paris Salon. It was not only the most expensive Ferrari yet offered but also the fastest, with a genuine (and mind-boggling) top speed of 174 mph. Apart from the Lamborghini Countach, it was arguably the quickest road car in history. Its engine was the quad-cam 4.4-liter V-12 with 320 bhp at 7500 rpm. There were six

40 DCN 20 carbs, dry-sump lubrication, and five-speed transaxle. The prototype was designed and built by Pininfarina, with production carried out by Scaglietti.

Initially, the Daytona's nose was distinguished by a full-width wraparound plastic cover for the quad headlights. This gave way in mid-1971 to hidden headlights, which cleaned up front end appearance considerably. Despite hood, doors and trunklid made of aluminum, it was a heavy car, weighing in at over 3600 pounds, and detractors say it was heavy to drive. But this didn't affect the well-balanced chassis, and with the available horsepower and

torque the Daytona's performance was stunning. So, too, was the styling, though not everyone liked the long front end, truncated greenhouse, and short Kamm tail. Yet the functional, aggressive lines have aged quite well, and even those who criticized the styling originally have come to like it.

A year after the Daytona's debut a convertible version, the 365 GTS/4, was exhibited at Frankfurt. The factory announced only 15 would be built, but this wasn't enough to satisfy demand, and ultimately some 150 were built. In recent years this number has been increased substantially as many berlinetta owners have

Below and right: The 365 California Spyder, Ferrari's grand luxe *convertible for 1966. Bottom and center spread: The 365 GT 2+2. A U.S. magazine called it Ferrari's "sedan."*

had their cars converted, in part because the spyder commands a higher price on the collector market.

A number of competition Daytonas have also been prepared, but were never officially campaigned by the factory. Although production ceased in 1973, Daytonas could still be seen on the grids at some long-distance events years afterward. In racing trim, it could top 200 mph. Today, a Daytona in top condition can cost up to $30,000, the racing ones even more (assuming their owners are willing to part with them). Total production (berlinetta and spyder) is estimated at around 1350.

Replacing the 330/365GTC as the luxury two-seat Ferrari was the 365 GTC/4, introduced at Geneva in March 1971. Although it had two small back seats, it would strain credulity to call this a genuine 2+2. Its engine was similar to the Daytona's, but used six Weber 38 DCOE sidedraft

Left and lower left: The 365 GTB/4, dubbed Daytona by the press shortly after its late-1968 debut. Early covered headlamps gave way to hidden lamps in 1971. Below: The Daytona at Daytona. A number were campaigned by privateers but never by the factory. Bottom: The highly coveted 365 GTS/4, the Daytona Spyder, debuted at Turin 1969.

carbs feeding manifolds incorporated in the cam covers. The first Ferrari engine designed with the U.S. market in mind, it was not only wider but lower than the Daytona's powerplant, which allowed a low, sloping hoodline with room enough to house the necessary anti-pollution gear. Unlike the Daytona, the five-speed gearbox in the 365GTC/4 was bolted directly behind the engine. Of course, there was the obligatory all-independent suspension and four-wheel disc brakes. Because of its considerable weight, the car also had standard ZF power steering. Somehow this model didn't have the exciting style expected in a Ferrari, but it was clean-lined and understated, and had all the accoutrements appropriate for a luxury GT.

In 1972 a ritzy four-seater, the 365 GT4 2+2, was unveiled. Powered by the now familiar 4390cc (267.9-cid) V-12, it was mechanically similar to the GTC/4 but had a 200mm (7.87-inch) longer wheelbase. About 470 were made. By this time, Ferrariphiles must have been wondering what would happen next. Maranello's road machines had long ago ceased being thinly disguised racers. Comfort, even luxury had taken over: power steering, air conditioning, radio, and other refinements once considered unthinkable had now become necessities. The surprise for the 1976 Paris Salon was the first Ferrari with standard automatic

This page, top and above: Considered plain when new, the lines of the 365 GTC/4 have aged well. Pop-up headlamps were a new feature. Upper right and right: Launched in 1972, the 365 GT4 2+2 was the four-seat companion to the GTC/4. Both were powered by the 4.4-liter Colombo V-12. Page opposite: The 365 GT4's engine was punched out to 4.9 liters for the renamed but otherwise little changed 400 model in 1976. Below: The neat convertible conversion of the 400Ai by Straman of California.

120

transmission. This was basically the 365 GT4 2+2 with an engine enlarged to 4823cc (294.3 cid). There were two versions, the 400 GT with five-speed manual shift and the 400 A with a three-speed General Motors Turbo-Hydramatic. The 400 is still in production at this writing, and retains its predecessor's Pininfarina notchback coupe styling. Seats were redesigned to slide forward on their tracks when the backrest is tilted forward to provide easier entry/exit for rear seat passengers. A quadraphonic stereo radio/cassette system is standard equipment. On the outside, a small front spoiler was added for the 400, taillights were redesigned, and the driver's door got a remote-control mirror. There were also new Cromodora wheels with five-lug mounting instead of the previous center-lock knock-off hubs. The 400 has not been certified by the factory to meet current American regulations and is thus not sold here. However, a few have been imported after being brought into compliance by various firms specializing in legalizing high-buck Italian exotics. One California outfit not only modifies the 400 for sale, but also offers a very slick and handsome convertible conversion of this model. Like all current Ferraris, the 400 now has fuel injection (Bosch K-Jetronic), making its designation the 400i. Manual gearbox is no longer offered.

THE MID~ENGINE V~12 SPORTS/ RACING CARS

The ultimate development of the successful mid-engine 330 P series was the 330 P4 of 1967.

During 1960 Ferrari began experimenting with the rear-/mid-engine layout in his single-seat V-6 Dinos, which appeared in a number of Formula 1 and 2 races. He was soon convinced this would be the wave of the future for grand prix, sports/racing, and GT cars. Indeed, several constructors, notably Lotus, had pioneered this configuration. After 1961 there would be no more front-engine racing Ferraris.

It was not until late 1962 that any thought had been given to using a V-12 behind the driver. That's when John Surtees began testing a Dino 246 SP fitted with a 3.0-liter Testa Rossa engine. This car was entered in the 1963 Targa Florio, but was badly damaged by fire. The first mid-engine prototype to emerge from Maranello was the 250 P, which Ferrari displayed at a special press show in March 1963. From then until the early 1970s the berlinetta and spyder sports/racing cars campaigned by the factory and various private teams were all V-12 powered. Two 250 Ps were sent to Sebring for the 12-hour race in March 1963. They finished 1st and 2nd, with John Surtees/Lodovico Scarfiotti and Mairesse/Vaccarella doing the honors. Four of these 2953cc (180.2-cid) cars were built. At the 1963 Paris Salon it was apparent that they were the prototypes for the new 250 LM (Le Mans). Listed as a catalog model designed primarily for competition, the 250 LM was intended for the 3.0-liter GT class even though its actual displacement was above the specified limit, 3285cc (200.5 cid). For this reason, the FIA didn't homologate the model until 1966, and by then it was too late. Because of its engine size, it should have been designated a 275, which, of course, wasn't what Ferrari had in mind. Some 40 examples were built. All had the odd-number chassis identification indicating the factory considered them roadgoing GTs. The 250 LMs were raced by private customers (including Luigi Chinetti's North American Racing Team) at Daytona, Sebring and in SCCA National

This page, above: The 250/330P as seen at a California concours in the early '70s. Right and page opposite: The mid-engine 250 LM was clearly designed for competition, but many were also used on the road.

events. The factory also ran them, winning no less than 10 major events in 1964.

The 275 P followed, and was similar in most respects to the 250 LM. Bore and stroke were the same 77 x 58.8mm (3.03 x 2.31 inches) for the 3285cc twin-cam engine with one plug per cylinder and six Weber 38 DCN carburetors. A five-speed rear transaxle and all-independent suspension were also retained.

The main difference was an increase in rated power from 305 bhp at 7500 rpm on the LM to 320 bhp at 7700 rpm. The 275 P was introduced in 1964 for factory use at the same time as the 330 P (the latter with a displacement of 3967cc/242.1 cid). Clarification of chassis numbers between these two is partly guesswork as the engines of both prototypes were interchangeable.

The 275 P2 and 330P2 were introduced in 1965. The former had the same displacement as the 275 P but gained the quad-cam head with two plugs per cylinder. The latter was similar to the 330 P, but its engine got the same treatment, which boosted power to 410 bhp at 8500 rpm. Both these sports prototypes were Ferrari's answer to the mounting threat from the mid-engine Ford GT. It is interesting to note that these four-cam powerplants were based on the 290, 315, and 412 series of sports/racing engines dating back to 1957. Also in 1965 Ferrari came up with the 365P2

This page: Apart from the prototype, all 250 LMs had a 3.3-liter engine. Ferrari should have called it a 275, but wanted the model homologated for the 3.0-liter GT class. Page opposite: A 250 LM owned by GM stylist Henry Haga (upper left) is flanked by the 365 P2/3 (upper right) and 330 P3 (below) endurance racers.

and 365P2/3 for non-factory teams (NART, Maranello Concessionaries, and Ecurie Francorchamps were three of the most prominent). Displacement here was 4390cc/267.9 cid (81 x 71mm/3.19 x 2.79 inches) for 380 bhp at 7300 rpm.

All the sports prototypes beginning with the 250 P were reasonably successful in competition. They also illustrate an interesting point. Although Ferrari was the leading sports/GT constructor in 1962-65 and again in 1967 and '72, it seldom built an all-new car. The power unit, gearbox, or suspension might be revised, but not all at the same time. This reflected the factory's concern with thorough development as well as its willingness to experiment.

In 1966 came a development of the 330P2 logically dubbed 330P3, incorporating a number of new or revised mechanical features. The clutch was relocated between engine and gearbox instead of directly behind the transmission, which was now a five-speed ZF unit, and Lucas fuel injection substituted for the customary Weber carbs. While

the major portion of the body was still aluminum, fiberglass panels were used for the first time. Like its predecessors, the 330P3 was a low-slung, svelte, but aggressive-looking car. Its 3967cc (242.1-cid) engine produced an impressive 420 bhp at 8000 rpm. It was hoped this car would keep the Fords at bay during the 1966 season, especially at Le Mans where Ferraris had always been odds-on favorites. Prospects for a Ferrari victory in the 24-hour race seemed bright after an easy

win by Mike Parkes and Lodovico Scarfiotti in the Spa-Francorchamps 1000km in May. But hopes faded due to labor problems at the factory that hindered car preparation, plus a quarrel between racing manager Eugenio Dragoni and driver John Surtees, who walked out before the race. (It wasn't their first altercation; Surtees had accused Dragoni before of showing favoritism to the team's Italian drivers.) As most enthusiasts know, Fords won this race in a

stunningly impressive display. The remainder of the season was not a happy one for Ferrari, and some of the 330P3s were sold to private buyers.

During December 1966 the replacement 330P4 was tested at Daytona with a new engine designed by Franco Rocchi. While displacement was the same 3967cc as in the 330P2/P3, this engine incorporated three valves per cylinder (two intake and one exhaust) and the Lucas fuel injection fed induction tubes mounted between the camshafts instead of on the inside of the cylinder banks. There were two spark plugs per cylinder and four coils. On an 11:1 compression ratio, this unit was rated at a massive 450 bhp at 8200 rpm. The ZF transmission was replaced by a factory designed and built unit.

The P4 was the final development of the 330 P series, and was derived from the Formula 1 cars seen at Monza. Some minor chassis changes were made to accommodate wider tires (made by Firestone, under contract to Ferrari). Two cars were entered for the Daytona Continental in February 1967, the test car, a spyder, for Chris Amon and Lorenzo Bandini and a berlinetta for Scarfiotti and Parkes. Other Ferraris present were a NART P3 (brought up to P4 specification but with carburetors) for Pedro Rodriguez/Jean Guichet, a similar Ecurie Francorchamps entry for Mairesse/Beurlys, and the David Piper P2/3. NART also

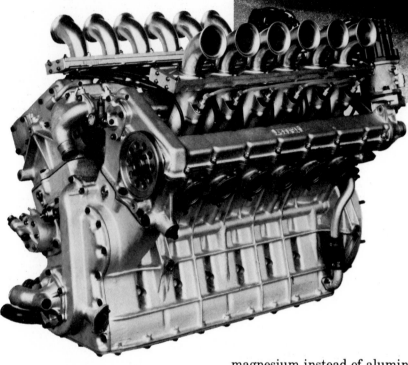

Right and below: The rakish 330 P4 endurance racer and its magnificent-looking V-12 powerplant. A squadron of P4s was ultimately defeated at Le Mans 1967 by Ford's Mark IV GTs, though it was a close contest.

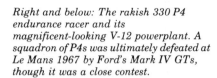

entered a Drogo-bodied 365 P2 for Masten Gregory and Jo Schlesser. Ferrari dominated the race. To humiliate the Fords, which had lined-up three across at the Le Mans finish the previous year, the two works 330 P4s and the NART P3 crossed the line in tandem. On their home ground at Monza, 330 P4s placed 1st and 2nd in the 1000 kilometers, but the sole entry at Spa could not do better than 5th. Another P4 contested the Targa Florio, but the usually sound Vaccarella hit a wall on his home circuit, breaking the two right side wheels. To prepare for the "big one" at Le Mans, Ferrari sat out the long-distance Nurburgring event.

Four factory 330 P4s were entered for Le Mans '67, all with magnesium instead of aluminum transmission housings, which gave a weight saving of 30 lbs per car. Also on the grid were the 330 P3/P4s (now with the Ferrari-designed five-speed transmission) campaigned that season by NART, Maranello Concessionaires, and Scuderia Filipinelli, plus a 365 P2/3, also from NART. The Ferraris' biggest challengers were American: Ford's Mark IV and Jim Hall's Chaparral. After eight hours, the Fords of Dan Gurney, Bruce McLaren, and Mario Andretti plus Scarfiotti's P4 berlinetta were all on the same lap. At 2 a.m. Andretti's brakes locked in the esses, and the Roger McCluskey and Jo Schlesser Fords crashed trying to avoid it. During the long night, the Foyt/Gurney Ford built up a long lead over the Parkes/Scarfiotti P4, with the Chaparral in 3rd. In the final two hours on Sunday, the Ferrari gained 10 seconds a lap on Foyt/Gurney, but the Ford had enough speed and stamina to cross the finish line first.

The BOAC 500 at Brands Hatch in July was the last round in the 1967 Manufacturers' Championship. The Phil Hill/Mike Spence Chaparral won, but a 2nd place (the 330 P4 driven by Chris Amon/Jackie Stewart) gave Ferrari the constructors' crown by a slim two point margin over Porsche, with Ford in 3rd place. Ferrari had won the championship for the twelfth time in 14 years. It should be noted that the correct designation for the 330 P3/4 should be 412P. These were 330 P3s brought up to 330 P4 specification but with Weber carbs instead of Lucas fuel injection. Four examples were built for the various independents already mentioned.

In the summer of 1967 the FIA decreed new displacement limits for 1968: 3.0 liters for prototype cars and 5.0 liters for sports cars. The FIA, always a law unto itself, often made sudden, unpredictable rule changes that gave constructors little time to comply. The decision certainly didn't suit Enzo Ferrari, but he could be just as unpredictable. At first he said he would not build any cars for

Above: The 312 P was created for the 1968 3.0-liter formula for prototype sports cars. Jackie Ickx is shown driving an early example at Brands Hatch in '68.

the new 3.0-liter formula, but then displayed the 250 P5 at Geneva 1968. This car had a displacement of 2990cc/182.5 cid (77 x 53.5mm/3.03 x 2.11 inches) plus four-cam head, two plugs per cylinder, five-speed transaxle, and Lucas injection. It was, in fact, a show car but predicted the 312P announced in December. Specifications were similar except for a single plug and four valves per cylinder, and a 2370mm (93.3-inch) wheelbase versus 2380mm (93.7) for the 250 P5. It was designed and engineered by Calari (in charge of aerodynamics), Rocchi (who worked on the power unit) and Marelli (the development engineer), with Mauro Forghieri overseeing the whole project. A development of the 3.0-liter Formula 1 car, the 312P was seen in both berlinetta and spyder form during the 1969 Manufacturers' Championship. A

very fast car, it won the pole position in the six races it entered. It also led some races for a time or was well up in the field before retiring. At season's end its record read only two 2nds and one 4th. The factory campaigned it for just a single season. It is believed three were built (chassis numbers 0868, 0870, and 0872). All were sold off, but some saw action in 1970-71 in the hands of NART and other independents.

At the time the 312P was in the works Ferrari was also busy preparing for the new 5.0-liter sports car class and, of course, the usual Formula 1 program. Once more Enzo had fallen into his old trap of trying to do too much for his available resources. The new sports car formula stipulated a

minimum of 50 cars for homologation. Both Porsche and Ferrari protested, the officials had second thoughts, and the required number was lowered to 25.

Turin 1969 saw a *speciale* Ferrari show car by Pininfarina on a new chassis designated 512. At Geneva the following March was an even wilder mid-engine design on this platform called the Modulo. Neither was meant for either road or track, but they did herald the December arrival of the new 5.0-liter competition sports car, the 512S. Though it wasn't nearly as futuristic in appearance as the show cars, this new long-distance contender looked like no other Manufacturer's Championship Ferrari ever built. Along with the way-out Porsche 917, it signalled a return to the kind of racing where the giants battle it out with brawny, blistering,

big-displacement cars.

The 512S had been conceived in April 1969, and its development was reportedly backed by Fiat (which bought control of the Ferrari company that year). Three works cars would be fielded for 1970 to regain the Manufacturers' Championship. Other examples would be sold to favored independents. The engine was based on castings used for the Type 612, created for the Canadian-American Challenge Cup series. With its reduced capacity it was thought this engine would hold up well in European endurance events. Its design was in the Ferrari mold, a

60-degree V-12 with twin overhead camshafts per bank, four valves and a single 10mm plug per cylinder. Displacement was 4994cc/304.8 cid (87 x 70mm/3.43 x 2.76 inches). Four fuel pumps driven by the right intake camshaft fed the indirect Lucas injection system, and the single Marelli distributor was driven by the left intake camshaft from the rear of the engine. Radiators were mounted on both sides of the car and an oil cooler was located in the nose. The crankcase and many engine parts were light-alloy castings. The engine sat behind the driver and ahead of a rear transaxle with

This page, above: The 312 P long-distance racer, photographed at Maranello in early 1973. Page opposite: Ferrari's big-bore GT endurance racer in the early '70s was the 512 S with a midships-mounted V-12. Car shown below has the early short-tail bodywork, while the one above has the later style with better high-speed stability.

five-speed all-synchro gearbox and limited-slip differential. The clutch was a multi-disc unit. Disc brakes were from Girling, and had no servo assistance. The frame was tubular steel on a wheelbase of 2400mm (94.5 inches). Campagnolo center-lock alloy wheels were specified, shod with Firestone tires. Suspension was all-independent, with

unequal-length A-arms at the front, reversed lower arms at the rear for wheel alignment, plus coil springs and Koni shock absorbers at each corner. Steering was rack-and-pinion.

The 512S went through five different body alterations. The first had a white louvered panel over the engine compartment and an upswept tail with a hint of spoiler. Headlights were located in the front of the fenders, and two driving lights were placed low in the middle of the nose. For its debut race at Daytona in late January 1970, the car had a modified tail with fins and a larger spoiler. Five berlinettas were entered, three by the factory and one each by NART and Scuderia Picchio Rosso. The only finisher was the Andretti/Merzario/Ickx factory car, in 3rd place behind two Gulf Porsches. For Sebring in March, the factory entered a berlinetta and two spyders; NART had a third spyder. To improve frontal stability, noses were lowered and given a blunt square profile. Also, scoops were added to cool the fuel pumps, addressing a problem that had surfaced at Daytona. Modifications to the injection system produced an additional 40 bhp, bringing overall output to a hefty 590 bhp. A few chassis changes reduced overall weight by nearly 88 lbs. Once more there was only one finisher, the berlinetta handled by Vaccarella/Giunti/Andretti, but it took 1st place. For the Monza 1000km, two berlinettas and a spyder were listed. They finished 2nd, 3rd and 4th, with a Gulf Porsche again taking 1st. A win also evaded the 512S in the Spa and Nurburgring events.

Then came Le Mans, which proved a disaster. There were 11 Ferraris in the running. The factory had entered four 512S cars with revised *coda lunga* (long-tail) bodywork. There were two similar cars entered by

Scuderia Filipinetti plus a lone Belgian entry. Three private entrants stayed with the standard 512S body, and NART had a 312P as its second car. It seemed that Ferrari should have won on numbers alone, and it might have had it not been for a pileup in the

This page, below: The 512 S competed at the last Daytona 24 Hours in January 1971. This particular car was entered by the North American Racing Team. Driven by Bucknum/Adamowicz, it placed second overall. Page opposite: The later 512 M (Modified) takes a corner at the twisty Laguna Seca course in a Ferrari Owners Club race in 1974. Note roof blister to provide clearance for the driver's head.

rain in the early hours. It happened when Reine Wisell slowed his 512S because oil on the windshield had reduced his visibility. Clay Regazzoni and then Michael Parkes hit him, and in the resultant confusion Derek Bell overturned, thus putting four Ferraris out of contention. Then, the engine in the Giunti/Vaccarella car failed, privateers Loos/Kelleners retired with a badly damaged nose, and the Moretti/Manfredini car lost its gearbox lubricant. Ickx and Schetty were in 3rd place after 9 hours when a rear brake locked. The car went off the course,

fatally injuring a marshall before it burst into flames. Juncadella's 512S then split its gearbox casing. In the midst of all these setbacks three Ferraris did manage to survive: the NART car (Posey/Bucknum) in 4th, the Belgian entry 5th, and the NART 312P (Adamowicz/Parsons) unplaced for covering too few miles.

With the final 1970 championship round looming for the Osterreichring in Austria, Ferrari produced the 512M (M for modified). This car had a revised aerodynamic body with a carburetor air scoop at the rear of the roof and a shorter tail to which small adjustable wings were added. It also had engine and suspension changes. The 512M easily outdistanced the Porsches early in the race and set a new lap record, but the sole works entry, driven by Ickx and Giunti, went out with electrical troubles. Later in the year two cars went to South Africa for the Kyalami race, where Ickx and Giunti took the pole and were never headed. Bell and De Fierlandt driving a Belgian 512S finished 6th.

But Ferrari was finished with the disappointing 512S. All but one, a 512M (chassis no. 1010), were sold to parties in America and Europe who raced them extensively, but without much success. The remaining car was sent to Imola for a 300-kilometer race in May 1970, where Merzario came home in 1st. Of the S types, 10 were updated to M specification, and four more were converted by their owners. A number of 512s are still around, and some are seen in vintage races. These include the Roger Penske/Kirk White 512M, a car which was always immaculately prepared and quite probably the fastest of its type.

THE CAN-AM CARS

The Canadian-American Challenge Cup, instituted in 1966, was a special series for Group 7 cars. Events were staged on both U.S. and Canadian tracks, and attracted a large number of American and European entries, professional and amateur. The schedule usually ran from early September to the end of November. The torquey and powerful 7.0-liter Chevrolet V-8 was the engine most popular with Can-Am hopefuls, which made Ferrari's arrival for 1967 a surprise.

Luigi Chinetti, the American Ferrari distributor and backer of the North American Racing Team, had decided to enter the Can-Am. Accordingly, he sent his 330P3/4 (412P) back to Italy to have it prepared. Though it's doubtful any mechanical modifications were made to this car, its overall weight was reduced and its body was given a lower profile. Its first race was at Bridgehampton in September. Lodovico Scarfiotti took it to 7th place, a satisfactory finish against tough opposition from the Chevy-powered Lolas and McLarens. Scarfiotti was left on the grid at Mosport, then got going but didn't finish.

Meanwhile, Maranello began taking an interest in the series, and prepared a couple of Group 7

prototypes based on the 330P4. These were lightened, and engine displacement was increased to 4176cc (254.8 cid) (79 x 71mm/3.11 x 2.79 inches) for 480 bhp at 8500 rpm. Bill Harrah, the hotel magnate and a Ferrari dealer, sponsored these cars, designated 350 CanAm/350P4, which enjoyed full factory support. Chris Amon and Jonathan Williams drove them to 5th and 8th places, respectively, at Laguna Seca against the more powerful opposition. At Riverside, Amon took 9th place, but Williams spun out of the race after a shunt from Peter Revson's Lola-Chevrolet. The Ferrari twosome finished the season at the Stardust Grand Prix in Las Vegas, but neither car finished the race.

Mauro Forghieri, Ferrari's competition engineer, seemed duly satisfied with the promise of his "underpowered" cars. But clearly, something like a 6.0-liter engine would be needed to win. The result was a new car designed specifically for the Can-Am. Displacement was pegged at 6221cc/379.6 cid (92 x 78mm/3.62 x 3.07 inches). The big V-12 had Ferrari's usual quad cams, four valves and two plugs per cylinder, plus Lucas indirect fuel injection. A four-speed gearbox in unit with the differential was fitted. With 620 bhp at 7000 rpm, the new 612 was eagerly awaited throughout the 1968 season, but it arrived only for the final round at Las Vegas. Even then it didn't complete one lap: Chris Amon was involved in a first-turn pileup

that put all the leaders out of contention.

The 612 was reworked some for the 1969 season. At Watkins Glen, Amon took 3rd place behind the McLarens of Denis Hulme and Bruce McLaren, following up at Edmonton by a 2nd place finish only five seconds behind Hulme. A piston collapsed in practice for the Mid-Ohio contest, so the one and only 612 engine had to be returned to Italy. There were no backup engines available stateside, an indication perhaps that the factory was only "playing" with this project. This left only the underpowered 1968 engine, but Amon managed a fine 3rd place behind the very competitive McLarens. The 6.2-liter unit was returned for the Michigan race, but a rod bearing failed during a late practice session, leaving Amon in the pits. The car was again a non-starter at Laguna Seca, where an oil pump packed up during the time trials. The factory sent over a 6.9-liter (421.1-cid) engine in time for the Riverside run. This was installed in the 612 chassis to create what should have been called a 712. Again the qualifying session revealed problems, this time with oil cooling, but Amon did post third-fastest time. On race day, October 26, the car's starter failed at the green flag. After a push-start, which was ruled illegal, Amon was black-flagged, and once more his race was run before it had begun. The "712" was then sent to Texas International Raceway for the final event. A failed piston forced Amon into the 612, which retired after completing a mere 10 laps.

In all, Ferrari's assualt on the Can-Am was a very half-hearted one. Amon enjoyed little close factory support, and even had to form his own team of mechanics just to look after the cars from race to race. As mentioned, the 612 engine castings later became the basis for the 512 S powerplant, but this was about the only tangible result from the factory's brief foray into big-bore racing.

The 350 Can Am/350P4 in one of its early outings. It led to the Type 612, campaigned without much success in 1968-69.

THE FRONT V~6 SPORTS/RACING CARS

Ferrari had participated in Formula 2 with considerable success beginning in 1949-51 with the 1955cc (121.7-cid) 166F2 V-12 car. When the FIA decreed that Formula 2 would decide the 1952-53 Manufacturers and Drivers World Championships, Aurelio Lampredi produced the 1980cc (120.8-cid) Type 500F2 with an inline four-cylinder engine. Ferrari took the Manufacturers Championship and Alberto Ascari the Drivers Championship with this car in both years.

In 1956 Ferrari was looking ahead to new Formula 2 regulations for 1957-58. The upper displacement limit was set at 1500cc unsupercharged, and while commercial fuel would have to be used for 1957, higher-octane aviation fuel would be allowed for 1958. Vittorio Jano and his design team were ordered to devise a new range of V-6 engines to meet this formula. The first to appear was the Dino 156F2, piloted in its inaugural running in the Naples Grand Prix by Luigi Musso in April 1957. Though the race was for Formula 1 cars, he finished 3rd behind Peter Collins and Mike Hawthorn driving 2.5-liter Ferrari/Lancia 801s.

There were to be three distinct families of Dino V-6s that would see duty in Formula 1, Formula 2, sports/racing, and GT cars. Jano designed the first two, Franco Rocchi the third. Ferrari's son Alfredo was in on the early discussions regarding these engines, and it was this association that led Enzo to call them (and, later, some cars) by his son's nickname, Dino. There was also a different numbering system for these engines in which the first two figures denoted

displacement in liters and the third digit the number of cylinders. Thus the 156 had a 1.5-liter six; similarly, the 196 S sports/racing car had a 1.9-liter six.

Ferrari's front-engine V-6 sports/racing cars made only a few track appearances. While there were four different types, only six were built in all. The first Dino appeared at Goodwood in England in April 1958. Driven by Peter Collins, it placed 2nd behind the Stirling Moss Aston Martin DBR2. This Dino 206 S had a 65-degree included angle and a displacement of 1983cc/121.0 cid (77 x 71mm/3.03 x 2.79 inches) plus twin overhead camshafts for each cylinder bank, two plugs per cylinder, and three Weber 42 DCN carburetors. Power was quoted at 220 bhp at 8500 rpm. The drivetrain layout

Above: The 246 F1 car at speed. Below: The heart of the 246 F1 was this light but strong tubular chassis.

was the usual Ferrari type, with a live rear axle, coil springs front and rear, and four-speed gearbox directly behind the engine. Only one was built. Its only other outing was the Grand Prix of Naples, where it retired with an ailing clutch, but not before Musso had set the fastest lap.

The Dino 296 S was introduced at Silverstone about a month after the 206 S. Mike Hawthorn was at the wheel, but he had to be content with 3rd place behind two Lister-Jaguars. The 296 S didn't race again until 1960, when it reappeared completely reworked with an extended 2320mm (91.3-inch) wheelbase, V-12 engine, and five-speed gearbox. Steering was transferred from left to right in a new body designed by Fantuzzi. Luigi Chinetti bought this car for the Rodriguez brothers, who took it to 3rd place at Sebring 1961.

Enzo Ferrari felt these first Dinos were too expensive and too complicated to sell to private customers. Initially he had planned to build them strictly for factory use, then changed his mind. The next two cars in this series, the 196 S and 246 S, had

the simpler twin-cam head and single plug per cylinder. However, it's a little difficult to understand all this because apparently only two of each were built, which would hardly suggest a serious attempt at a customer race car. In other respects, the 196

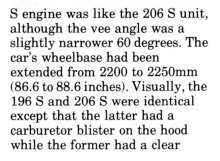

A rare closeup look at the Dino 246 Formula 1 car from 1960. As its designation indicates, this car's engine displacement was close to 2.4 liters. The engine itself was a V-6 with Ferrari's favored 60-degree included angle between cylinder banks. Despite a well-chosen design, the 246 S did not meet with much success, and gave way after only a single season to new mid-engine sports/racing designs.

V-6 but with less displacement, 2417cc (147.5 cid). Also like the 196 S, it did not have much success. Its best effort was a 4th in the 1960 Targa Florio.

Bodywork for all four of these Dinos was designed by Pinin Farina, but construction was given to Carrozzeria Fantuzzi mainly because Ferrari's usual contractor, Scaglietti, was already busy building cars like the 250 GT swb models. But Enzo Ferrari didn't pay much, if any, attention to development of these "first wave" V-6 cars despite what you might think from his use of his son's name. The Testa Rossas and the World Sports Car Championship, not to mention Formula 1, were of more interest to *Il Commendatore* at this time.

S engine was like the 206 S unit, although the vee angle was a slightly narrower 60 degrees. The car's wheelbase had been extended from 2200 to 2250mm (86.6 to 88.6 inches). Visually, the 196 S and 206 S were identical except that the latter had a carburetor blister on the hood while the former had a clear plastic cover open to the front. The 196 S compiled a dismal racing record. Transmission trouble, a blown engine, and rear axle failure marred the '59 season, and 1960 was little better.

The last front-engine Dino, the 246 S, was first seen in action at Buenos Aires in January 1960. Like the 196 S, it had a 60-degree

THE MID~ENGINE V~6 SPORTS/ RACING CARS

The year 1961 saw the racing world turn from the front-engine configuration to the mid-/rear-engine layout. Enzo also knew that this was the way he had to go if he wanted to keep in contention. Accordingly, three mid-engine prototype sports cars were built between 1961 and 1962. The first was the Dino 246 SP, introduced at a press conference in February 1961. Its 65-degree quad-cam V-6 had a capacity of 2417cc/147.5 cid (85 x 71mm/3.35 x 2.79 inches) and was rated at 270 bhp at 8000 rpm. A five-speed gearbox was in unit with the differential as a transaxle. This car's first race was the Sebring 12-hours, where Richie Ginther and Wolfgang Von Trips had it in the lead until a steering arm broke. Two cars were fielded for the Targa Florio for Ginther/Hill and Von Trips/Gendebien. There was a terrific duel between the Von Trips car and the Moss/Bonnier 2.0-liter Porsche in which the lap record was broken with monotonous regularity. Ultimately, Von Trips won after the Porsche's transmission failed on the final lap. At the Nurburgring 1000, rain got in through the engine cover louvers of both 246 SPs causing misfiring and spoiling any hope for a win. Nonetheless, Von Trips finished 3rd. At Le Mans, after 16 hours of racing, Von Trips ran out of fuel on the Mulsanne Straight, the result of bad pit management.

Two new mid-engine V-6 racers were shown in February 1962, the Dino 196 SP and Dino 286 SP. The latter never raced in this form, though a V-8 was later used

The mid-engine Dino 206S (left) lines up with the 330 P3 at Maranello in January 1966.

in its chassis. The 196 SP had a displacement of 1983cc (121.0 cid) for its 60-degree twin-cam engine. Only one car was built in 1962. Two more appeared the following year, one possibly a rebuilt 1962 268 SP, the other a reworked '61 246 SP. The 196 SP was entered in the 1962 Targa Florio for Lorenzo Bandini and Giancarlo Baghetti. Willy Mairesse and Olivier Gendebien handled a 246 SP. The third entry was a V-8 car,

the new 268 SP, with Phil Hill at the wheel. Though Baghetti damaged his car in a spinout, he finished 2nd overall and 1st in the 2.0-liter class. The 2.4-liter V-6 was the overall winner. A cracked sump plate leaked oil, causing the 196 SP to retire at Nurburgring. It was also a DNF at the Nassau

Speed Week. A 196 SP took part in the 1963 Targa Florio, but whether this was one of the reworked cars or the original one is not known. However, it nearly beat Bonnier's Porsche, missing by only 11 seconds. The 196 SP was without doubt a versatile competitor. It won the 1962

Below and far right: The Dino 286 SP, photographed in May 1962. Very similar in appearance to the companion 196 SP, this model never raced in its V-6 form, but was later fitted with a V-8. Below: The Dino 206 S (left), the 330/P3 and "friend" at Maranello.

European Hill Climb Championship, Lodovico Scarfiotti besting the Porsches by 11 points.

Ferrari's next mid-engine sports prototype was unveiled in 1965, the Dino 166 P with a 1592cc (97.1-cid) 65-degree V-6. Only one was built, and it failed to distinguish itself at Monza, Vallelunga, Nurburgring or Le Mans. However, fitted with an experimental 2.0-liter V-6, it won the European Hill Climb Championship, with Scarfiotti driving.

This 2.0-liter unit became the heart of the 206 S in 1966. Plans were to build 50 for homologation in Group 4, but due to industrial problems, which also affected production of Ferrari's road cars, only 18 were completed. There were a number of engine variations. Early cars had Weber carburetors; Lucas fuel injection was adopted later. Some had one

plug per cylinder, others two, and there were 18- and 24-valve heads. All these were 65-degree units with quad-cam heads, and produced about 218 bhp at 9000 rpm. These small machines really

Below: The Dino 206 SP of 1966 was Ferrari's competitor in the small-capacity sports/prototype racing class.

were gems with their bodies designed by Piero Drogo's Carrozzeria Sports Cars and obviously patterned after the large P3s and P4s. They had a sensuality never seen before on a Ferrari, and this was carried on by Pininfarina through the Dino 206/246GT road cars.

Unfortunately, the 206 S was

not a track star, and the factory seemed to take little interest in perfecting the design, so its race career was short-lived. Most of those built were ultimately sold. One car (chassis no. 004) is still seen regularly in hill climb competition in the U.K., and that same car is also a regular concours winner.

continued on page 161

275 GTB & 275 GTS

Above: the 275 GTB. Below: the
275 GTS (Spyder). These were
the first road-going Ferraris to
have all-independent suspension. 145

123 HJF

250GT LM

JM 265

This model should logically be known as the 275 LM because of its 3.3-liter engine, but Ferrari persisted in calling it 250GT LM since it was built for GT events like the 24 Hours of Le Mans. An extemely handsome mid-engine car, this example belongs to Richard Colton.

330 LMB

148

The 330 LMB was a one-off built for the prototype class in the 1962 championship series for GT cars. Outwardly, it resembled the GTO, but had a 4.0-liter engine of the type seen in the 400 Superamerica GTs. Its hood and nose were GTO-like, and the tail was unmistakably patterned after the 250 GT Berlinetta Lusso's. It was certainly a purposeful-looking car.

149

275 GTB

The early 275 GTB model had what came to be called the "short" nose while later examples were given a longer front. Both versions are very pleasing to the eye. Adding to their appearance was a new-style alloy wheel replacing the tradi-tional wires. These are among the most sought-after of Ferraris today.

330 GT 2+2

Although not popular when new, the 330 GT 2+2 was not only a comfortable *gran turismo* but an extremely fast one thanks to its 4.0-liter engine. The Mark I here has a four-headlamp treatment; the Mark II reverted to twin lamps. Among afficionados, this model is considered ordinary and lacking in Ferrari flair.

500 Superfast
& 365 GTC

154

Above: The 500 Superfast. Unlike earlier models that used this name, this was a "catalog" offering, though production was limited to just 36 units. Below: The 365 GTC, essentially a 4.4-liter version of the 330 GTC. Designed and built by Pininfarina, it was produced for just two years.

275 GTB

Early 275 GTBs had a single camshaft per cylinder bank, but a revised version, introduced at the 1966 Paris Salon, had a twin-cam head. The model's 3.3-litre engine featured dry-sump lubrication. Bodies were built by Scaglietti to a Pininfarina design. Production was large by Ferrari standards—more than 350 units.

365 GTB/4
Daytona

The 365 GTB/4 was first seen at the 1968 Paris Salon with headlamps exposed behind a full-width, wraparound plastic cover.

Appearance was improved in 1971 by adoption of paired retractable headlamps. More commonly known as the Daytona,

this model is already a classic in the eyes of most Ferrari enthusiasts. It is capable of stunning acceleration.

365 GTB/4
Daytona

The spyder version of the 365 GTB/4 Daytona, introduced in 1969, led many berlinetta owners to chop the tops off their own cars.

Dino competition-inspired show car was displayed at Turin in 1967.

V~6 GRAN TURISMOS

In view of its many racing and sports/racing V-6 cars, it's surprising Ferrari took so long to produce a roadgoing GT with this engine configuration. The first of the production V-6s was the 206GT, shown at Turin in 1967. It had the 65-degree 1987cc/121.3-cid powerplant (86 x 57mm/3.39 x 2.24 inches), with quad-cam head, single plug per cylinder, and three Weber 40 DCF carburetors, plus a five-speed transaxle and all-independent suspension with coil springs. Unlike the various mid-engine sports prototypes, the engine was placed transversely behind the passenger compartment instead of longitudinally. This petite, low-slung, beautifully proportioned berlinetta was designed by Pininfarina, and was similar in outline to the Drogo-bodied 206 S. Scaglietti built the bodies in aluminum. About 200 cars were built, all with closed coachwork, which was also surprising as the design lent itself to a spyder or targa treatment.

The 206GT was phased out in 1969. Its successor was the

161

Above and page opposite: The Dino 206 GT was a sensation when it hit the streets in 1967. Its mid-mounted V-6 also powered the front-engine Fiat Dinos (Spyder shown at right).

sensational Dino 246GT, the least expensive car ever to come from Ferrari, priced under $14,000. Ferrari was after the Porsche 911 buyer at that time, but although this Dino failed to put a big dent in Porsche sales, it was enthusiastically received in both Europe and the U.S. One obvious difference between it and the 206 was a displacement increase from 2.0 to 2.4 liters and a corresponding jump in rated power from 180 to 195 bhp. In the past, Ferrari block castings had been made of silumin, a silicon/aluminum alloy. But Fiat built this engine out of cast iron, and it proved more reliable than the all-alloy 206 unit. Overall length was greater since wheelbase was lengthened from

the 206's 2280mm (89.8 inches) to 2340mm (92.1 inches). Overall height was also greater, but it didn't spoil the flowing lines inspired by the earlier car. Scaglietti, as was usual, built the bodies, which were switched to steel construction with aluminum

panels. The cast iron engine block and steel body increased the 246 GT's overall weight by a hefty 400 pounds compared with its predecessor. This naturally affected performance, although the claimed top speed of 150 mph seemed reasonable.

There were three versions of the Dino 246 GT. The Type L or Series I saw a total of 357 examples, followed by 507 of the Type M or Series II. The final Type E or Series III brought with it a spyder model, the 246 GTS. Altogether, 2732 berlinettas and 1180 open cars were built. The Series III was the only 246 GT officially certified for U.S. sale.

Fiat also had its own Dino, two of them in fact. Introduced in late 1966, these cars were initially powered by a detuned version of the 2.0-liter Ferrari-designed V-6, but mounted up front and driving a live rear axle. Beginning in late 1969, rear suspension was switched from solid axle to fully independent geometry, and the 2.4-liter engine was substituted (with the aforementioned switch from aluminum to cast iron for the block). Toward the end of the production run, Ferrari took over engine assembly from Fiat.

This collaboration was quite beneficial for Ferrari, because it enabled Maranello to homologate its V-6 as a Formula 2 production engine by piggybacking on Fiat production. By contrast, the Fiat Dino was a low-volume sideline for the giant Turin automaker, as shown by the production totals: 1163 spyders and 3670 coupes with the 2.0 V-6, 420 and 2398 of the 2.4-liter cars. There were two body styles, a sleek 2+2 fastback styled by Bertone and a curvy two-seat spyder roadster by Pininfarina. Both coachbuilders also built their respective monocoque body/chassis, though the engineering was Fiat's.

Today, the Fiat Dinos are highly collectible and have excellent appreciation potential. Prices are still reasonable:

$10,000-$12,000 is about the most you should expect to pay for one in excellent condition. The later cars are preferred for their more reliable iron-block engine, better

Above: Dino competition show car shows off its gullwing doors. Design was not intended for production, but there was some carryover on the 206 GT road car. Below: The beautiful Dino 246 GT from 1969 was well-received the world over.

suspension, five-speed ZF gearbox, and more "practiced" construction.

The Dino 246 was discontinued in 1973. Its replacement was the Bertone-styled 308 GT4 2+2 with mid-mounted V-8 and somewhat dumpy lines. But the true successor to the lithe and lovely 246 was the two-seat 308 GTB.

A curious thing about both the 206 and 246 Dinos is that neither bore the famous prancing horse badge or the Ferrari name. The factory, in fact, seemed to take occasional umbrage at journalists who referred to the cars as "Ferrari Dinos." Perhaps for this reason, some enthusiasts shunned them for not being "true" Ferraris, but the more knowledgeable didn't care. Like their Fiat counterparts, the Dinos are very strong now on the collector market. An excellent-condition 206 GT will bring anywhere from $20,000 to $25,000. The same values apply to the 246 berlinettas, while the companion GTS will fetch $30,000-$40,000 in top condition.

In all, the Ferrari Dinos were among Maranello's most commercially successful road cars. They were and are fleet, sleek, sexy-looking thoroughbreds with fine road manners and that special panache only a Ferrari seems to possess. They wouldn't beat a capably driven Porsche 911 in a drag race, but their distinctive character continues to endear them to connoisseurs of fine cars.

THE INLINE FOUR
SPORTS/RACING CARS

The successful 750 Monza, beautiful even for a race car.

Ferrari's 2.0-liter V-12 Formula 2 cars had been almost invincible from 1949 to 1951. Despite this, Enzo was impressed by John Heath's four-cylinder Alta-engine HWM cars, which he felt might be a threat. The reason: the fours could run most races without having to refuel whereas the V-12s guzzled gas, necessitating time-wasting pit stops. Ferrari also guessed rightly that the FIA would run the 1952-53 World Championship based on 2.0-liter Formula 2 specifications. Lampredi had already been at work on two four-cylinder engines, a 2.0-liter (90 x 78mm/3.54 x 3.07 inches) and a 2.5 (94 x 90mm/3.70 x 3.54). Ferrari's first experimental four-cylinder sports car was completed in 1953. It had the 2.5 engine in either a 166 or 250 MM chassis topped by a spyder body from Vignale. One of these cars appeared at Monza in June along with a 3.0-liter four with a Lampredi-designed, Autodromo-built body. Ascari drove the latter machine, but blew its engine during practice. Mike Hawthorn's 3.0-liter powerplant was then transferred to Ascari's car, and the 2.5 was installed in the Vignale spyder for Hawthorn. This car was likely designated 625 TF. Little is known about it, expect that it was

probably meant for the 1953 Targa Florio, hence the TF suffix. Possibly three were built (based on known chassis numbers 0302 TF, 0304 TF, and 0306 TF). Two were sold to Robert Bonomi and Luis Milan, who took them to Argentina and raced them for a number of years.

The 3.0 engine was the second of Ferrari's inline fours. It displaced 2941cc/179.5 cid (102 x 90mm/4.02 x 3.54 inches), and had four overhead camshafts, two plugs per cylinder, coil ignition, dual Weber 45 DCOA/3 carburetors and four-speed transaxle. Rated bhp was 225 at 6800 rpm for what was designated the 735 S.

During the winter of 1953-54

This page and page opposite: The 750 Monza first raced in June 1954. It was the most successful and most durable of the four-cylinder Ferrari racers. Enzo's son Dino designed the body, which still looks sleek and elegant even after some 30 years.

work began on a new engine derived from the Type 555 Supersqualo four. Aluminum-alloy castings were used for the cylinder head and block, crankcase, and sump. Cast iron cylinder liners screwed into the head, and rubber O-rings at the base of the liners made a satisfactory water seal. Displacement was 2992cc (182.6 cid) for this quad-cam, twin-plug four. With two Weber 58 DCOA/3

carburetors, power output was 260 bhp at 6000 rpm. There was a four-speed (later five-speed) transaxle. The new model was designated 750 Monza. Two were entered for the *Gran Premio Supercortemaggiore* at Monza in June 1954. One, driven by Hawthorn and Umberto Maglioli, was involved in a race-long dual with a prototype 2.5 Maserati that blew up near the finish, leaving the win to the other Monza piloted by Gonzales/Trintignant. Both these cars had new bodies. Hawthorn's car was similar to the original Autodromo style. The Gonzales car's body was designed by Dino Ferrari, and this style would be retained for all subsequent

This page: The 500 Mondial did fairly well during its brief racing career in the mid-'50s. Car at right is one of two berlinettas built by Pinin Farina on this platform, and obviously related to the 375 MM. Page opposite: 860 Monza was a larger-engine derivative of the 750 Monza.

Monzas. Maglioli took one to the Rheims 12-hour event. After a poor start, he made up a lot of ground, but his gearbox gave up just as he was about to take the lead. The 750 Monzas competed in other races with moderate success.

A larger-engine Monza derivative, the 860, saw action at the Tourist Trophy in September 1955, driven by Eugenio Castellotti and Piero Taruffi. This was the first undersquare Ferrari engine (stroke greater than bore) with dimensions of 102 x 105mm (4.02 x 4.13 inches). Total displacement was 3431cc (209.4 cid), and maximum power output was 310 bhp at 6200 rpm. The 860 had only a few successes during its brief life as a factory racer. It placed 3rd in the 1955 Targa Florio. The next year it scored 1st and 2nd in the 12-hours of Sebring and a 1st in the Tour of Sicily, then went on to finish 2nd and 3rd behind a 290 MM

in the Mille Miglia.

The Formula 2 powerplant that took the 500 F2 cars to the 1952-53 Manufacturers and Drivers World Championships was the basis for a new engine, which was likely installed first in a 250 MM chassis. This new car, called 500 Mondial, was campaigned by the factory and independents in 1954-55. The

prototype debuted in a 12-hour race at Casablanca in December 1953; Alberto Ascari and Luigi Villoresi won in class and placed 2nd overall (behind a customer version of the 4.5-liter 375 MM driven by Piero Scotti). The Series I Mondial had a chassis layout similar to that of the Monza, with De Dion rear suspension and four-speed transaxle. Most of the

bodies were spyders designed and built by Pininfarina, and had a strong resemblance to those of the 4.5-liter V-12 cars. Farina also built one special long-nose body, which was sent to the States. This was supposed to be the prototype for the Series II Mondial, but that car's coachwork was ultimately penned by Dino Ferrari and executed by Scaglietti. The Series II had two Weber 45 DCOA/3 carburetors, five-speed transaxle, and an increase in rated horsepower from 160 to 170, both at 7000 rpm. A Type 553 F2 head replaced the 500 F2 head of the Series I cars. Though other changes were made to boost power and speed in the Series II, drivers were finding it increasingly difficult to match the superiority of the 2.0-liter Maseratis. One of the Mondial's last victories was a

first-in-class at the 1956 Sebring 12-Hours, with Porfirio Rubirosa and Jim Pauley co-driving.

While most Mondials were spyders, there were also two elegant berlinettas built on this platform. Pininfarina's was a scaled-down version of the 1953-54 375 MM. Vignale's design was similar to that of the 1953 166, 250, and 340 MM spyders, except for the roof.

Since the Mondial was having a hard time with the Maseratis, development work was started on a new 2.0-liter four-cylinder car, which became the 500 Testa Rossa. Lampredi had left Ferrari in the summer of 1955 to work for Fiat in Turin. The new engineering team now consisted of Vittorio Jano, Alberto Massimino, Luigi Bellantani, and Andrea Fraschetti. The new

sports/racer was shown at New York in April 1956, and made its racing debut the following June at the 1000km Supercortemaggiore. The 500TRs placed 1st, 2nd, and 4th, driven by Collins/Hawthorn, Fangio/Castellotti, and Gendebien/De Portago, respectively. All had bodies by Carrozzeria Touring, the design being similar to the Mondial and Monza spyders but with larger front wheel cutouts. These cars had a 1985cc (121.1-cid) displacement (90 x 78mm/3.54 x 3.07 inches), four overhead camshafts, two plugs per cylinder, two Weber 40 DCC/3 carburetors, and a four-speed gearbox behind the engine. Power was rated at 180 bhp at 7000 rpm.

In July, three cars ran at Le Mans 1956, with 2.5-liter engines either drived from or actual 625 F1 grand prix units. To comply with regulations the cars had to run as prototypes, so Ferrari called them 625 LM. Their main rivals, running in the production class, were the 3.4-liter Jaguar D-types and the 2.9-liter Aston Martin DBR. With less power, the 625 LM quite naturally trailed the Jaguars in maximum speed down the Mulsanne Straight, 144.7 versus 156.7 mph. However,

Below: The 500 Mondial in action in the mid-'50s. Only a handful were built. Bottom: A modified version of the four-cylinder 500 TRC. Bodywork is similar to that of the V-12 250 Testa Rossa that followed it.

the Trintignant/Gendebien Ferrari managed a creditable 3rd overall behind the winning Jaguar and the runner-up Aston.

Towards the close of 1956, Ferrari announced a new 500 TRC design to conform to FIA Appendix C, hence the type designation. It was lower than the 500TR by some three inches. The Scaglietti-built body had a rudimentary convertible top because the rules dictated it. A "customer" racer, the TRC was mechanically similar to the 500 TR. It should be noted that both retained most of the 500 Mondial engine, but cylinder heads were like those of the 500 F2 cars. They

also had stronger connecting rods and crankshaft assembly and a lighter flywheel. In its final form the 500 TR engine developed 180 bhp at 7000 rpm. John von Neumann, the Ferrari distributor in Los Angeles, was a TRC buyer, and wasted little time dropping a 3.5-liter 860 Monza engine into his car. He and Richie Ginther drove their rather exotic hybrid in a number of events.

The 500 TR/TRCs were the last of the four-cylinder sports models built around components from Ferrari's grand prix cars. They certainly had their share of successes, and showed the factory's flexibility and enterprise in building cars for specific races. But Ferrari went back to his beloved V-12 with his next project, the 250 Testa Rossa.

Ferrari also indirectly produced a four-cylinder *road* car. This was the ASA 1000, a rather half-hearted attempt at marketing a "baby Ferrari," built from 1962 to '67. It evolved from the 850cc (51.9-cid) "Ferrarina" engine designed in 1961, which was then taken over by the DeNora electrochemical company. The 1032cc (62.9-cid) ASA twin-cam four had exactly square bore-and-stroke dimensions (69 x 69mm/2.71 x 2.71 inches), and was mounted in a tubular chassis similar in design to Ferrari's own 250 GT, only on a smaller scale. Suspension geometry also followed Maranello practice. Two body styles were offered, a two-seat coupe with bodywork by Touring and a two-place convertible by Corbetta. Wheelbase was a diminutive 86.5 inches, 6 inches shorter than a VW Beetle's, and overall length was a petite 152.8 inches. The ASA had a rated 96 bhp (gross) to pull around its 1830 pounds, which worked out to an unspectacular 19 pounds/horsepower. There was no serious effort to sell or even improve the car or provide backup service for it. Total production ran to only about 100 units before the venture folded.

THE INLINE SIX
SPORTS/RACING CARS

A beautiful engine for a beautiful racing machine: The twin-cam six of the 121 LM.

During 1955, Enzo Ferrari decided to take on Mercedes-Benz in sports car racing with a new range of competition machines powered by an inline six-cylinder engine. His rationale for this configuration likely was that he already had experience with various fours, so it would be a simple matter to add two more cylinders for more power. However, the notion proved to be only a flash in the pan. Only two such models were designed, both constructed in the same period as the 500 Mondial.

The first six-cylinder engine was an extension of the 2.5 four from the 625 F1 car. This model, the 118 Le Mans, used the same bore and stroke (94 x 90mm/3.70 x 3.54 inches), but its added cylinders boosted displacement to 3747cc (228.7 cid). The twin overhead camshafts were driven from the front of the engine by gears. Three Weber 45 DCO/A3 carburetors were used, and two Marelli distributors sparked the 12 plugs. On a compression ratio of 8.75:1 this engine was rated at 280 bhp at 6400 rpm.

The first outing for the 118 LM was the Buenos Aires 1000 km race in January 1955. Driven by Froilan Gonzales and Maurice Trintignant, it ran with the leaders until Gonzales was disqualified for taking a short cut into the pits. In February, Piero Taruffi won the Tour of Sicily with this model. It would be the only outright victory in Europe for an inline-six Ferrari.

A squad of five six-cylinder cars was entered for the 1955 Mille Miglia. Four were 118 LMs. The fifth had a larger engine based on the 3.0-liter Monza four but with two extra cylinders and 4412cc (269.2 cid). This car, the 121 LM, was driven by Eugenio Castellotti. Although he beat Stirling Moss' Mercedes 300 SLR to the first control point at Ravenna by two minutes, he retired shortly afterwards with either engine problems or tire trouble. Taruffi's 118 LM led the race for a time, but retired after the oil pump gave out. Umberto

This page and page opposite: Developed as a competitor for the Jaguar D-Type in 1955, the 121 LM was not a big winner, though its looks still suggest otherwise. Photo at far right shows the restored example once raced by Ernie McAfee in action at Laguna Seca in August 1974.

Maglioli, however, managed 3rd place, and a factory test driver, Sergio Sighinolfi, came in 6th.

Five cars were fielded for Le Mans 1955. All would be out of the race before the halfway mark. Castellotti led for the first few hours in his 121 LM, putting quite a distance between himself and the rest of the pack. Then his clutch began to slip, which let Fangio's 300 SLR and Hawthorn's Jaguar D-Type slip past, and after four hours he parked the Ferrari, which was overheating. The Hill/Maglioli and Trintignant/Schell 121 LMs also

didn't last. Neither did the 750 Monzas of Lucas/Helde and Gregory/Sparken. As noted elsewhere, the race was marked by tragedy when Pierre Levegh's Mercedes crashed, killing 80 spectators. The Mercedes team withdrew, and Hawthorn went on to a very somber victory.

The final international race for the 121 LM was the Swedish Grand Prix for sports cars. The track surface was rough, which prevented Castellotti from fully exploiting his car's greater power to beat Fangio and Moss. Although he was undoubtedly fastest in the field, Castellotti had to be content with 3rd place behind the two German cars.

Altogether, only four 121 LMs were built. One subsequently went to Bill Doheny, and two rebodied cars were sold to Jim Kimberly and Tony Parravano. All three machines would race in the U.S. for several more years.

For some reason the 118 LM and 121 LM have been called "Super Mondial" and "Super Monza," presumably because their engines were larger and obviously more powerful developments of the ones in those models. The 121 LM was quite fast. In practice at Le Mans, Castellotti was timed at 175.6 mph down the Mulsanne Straight.

THE V-8 GRAN TURISMOS

The Dino 308 GT4, the first mid-engine Ferrari 2+2, in its initial 1973 form.

The first roadgoing Ferrari with V-8 power appeared at the 1973 Paris Salon. As a replacement for the Dino 246, the new 308 GT4 2+2 was also called a Dino, but the two looked nothing alike. For the first time in many years, Carrozzeria Bertone was given a Ferrari design commission (Scaglietti would, as usual, handle construction). The final shape, though pleasing, was hardly

exotic or even eye-catching, especially compared with Pininfarina's sensuously curved 206/246. In some ways, mechanical layout dictated the GT4's lines, for this was Ferrari's first mid-engine car with 2+2 seating and a transversely mounted engine. The result was a chunky wedge with a low, grille-less nose, lots of glass, and a sloping roofline terminating in a square-cut tail. The profile was

probably the car's most unflattering angle, where the long 2550mm (100.4-inch) wheelbase looked out of proportion against the shorter greenhouse above. Nevertheless, the 308 GT4 proved popular despite what the design critics said. And for the first time, a couple with two small children could all enjoy the high-speed delights of a Ferrari.

Besides its many other "firsts,"

Page opposite: This one-of-a-kind open-roof version of the 308 GT4 was built by the small Fly Studio coachbuilders strictly for show purposes. The somewhat ungainly roofline may have convinced the factory not to build copies. This page, above: the racy cockpit of a British-market 308 GTBi. Below: The 308 GT4 became a full-fledged Ferrari in 1976. Shown is the 1979 model in American-market trim.

the 308 GT4 also introduced a new Ferrari engine. This was a four-cam 90-degree V-8 with a displacement of 2926cc (178.5 cid) rated at a lusty 250 bhp at 7700 rpm. Drive was taken to the rear wheels through an all-indirect five-speed gearbox mounted behind the power unit, not underneath it as in some other mid-engine layouts. Suspension was all-independent by unequal-length A-arms, coil springs, and tubular shock absorbers at each corner. An anti-roll bar was fitted front and rear.

In 1975 a smaller-displacement companion model, the 208 GT4, was launched. It was intended mainly for the Italian market, where high taxes and fuel prices made cars over 2.0-liters prohibitively expensive to buy and operate. A bore reduction from 81 to 66.8mm (3.18 to 2.63 inches) yielded 1991cc (121.5 cid); stroke remained at 71mm (2.79 inches), making this Ferrari's second undersquare engine. With a rated 170 bhp at 7700 rpm, the 208 had a respectable top speed of 137 mph. Its 3.0-liter sister was capable of seeing about 156 mph.

The 308 GT4 continued into early 1980, when it was replaced as the "family" Ferrari by the Mondial 8. In 1976, the Dino badges were removed, and the

GT4s officially became full-fledged Ferraris, though some traditionalists did not approve.

Two years after the GT4 appeared, a two-seat model, the 308 GTB, was introduced, again at Paris. Unfavorable reaction to the 2+2's styling led Ferrari back to Pininfarina for this design, and it was a dandy. It was quickly hailed as one of the most aesthetically pleasing road cars ever seen, largely because it combined the best styling elements of two other PF stunners, the Dino 246 and the big flat-12 365 Berlinetta Boxer. Yet the styling was unique unto itself, which only added to the car's allure. Bodies were initially constructed of fiberglass, but adverse customer reaction to the idea of a "plastic Ferrari" prompted a switch to steel during 1977. As you'd expect, the GTB used the GT4's transversely mounted quad-cam V-8 and inline five-speed transaxle. Suspension design was also shared. Accentuating the purposeful yet graceful lines were beautiful five-spoke Cromodora alloy

wheels much like those of the fabled Daytona.

To supplement the two-seat berlinetta, Ferrari brought out an open version, the 308 GTS, at the 1977 Frankfurt auto show.

This page and page opposite: The 308 GTB (below left and right) was introduced in 1975. The targa-top GTS version (bottom left and right) appeared two years later. These mid-engine V-8 models have been the mainstay of Ferrari's U.S. lineup since the late '70s. Current versions feature Bosch electronic fuel injection.

Styling was little changed from the coupe's, the main difference being the removable one-piece panel over the cockpit and louvered covers for the rear side windows. More properly, this body style should be called a targa rather than a spyder, but then the designation would have been GTT, which didn't sound quite right. However, if you want your 308 to be a full convertible there

is a firm in Chicago, International Autos, that will perform the necessary surgery on your GTB or GTS or will sell you a ready-made car, which it calls the 308 GTR.

The 308 GTB and GTS have been the staples of Ferrari's U.S. lineup for the past several years. They offer outstanding performance and reasonably good passenger and luggage accommodation for mid-engine

two-seaters plus, as always, that special *elan* that is Ferrari's alone. The 308's image as a "fantasy" car has recently been bolstered (as if it needed to be) by a GTS seen regularly in the TV series "Magnum P.I." Both GTB and GTS remain in production at this writing essentially unchanged. The only mechanical alteration of note was made with the 1981 models, where Bosch K-Jetronic fuel injection replaced the four Weber DCNF carburetors previously used. These cars can be identified by the "i" suffix on the tail.

Meanwhile, the successor to the 308 GT4 was introduced in 1980 as the Mondial 8. Basically, this is a 2+2 derivative of the 308 GTB/GTS platform, sharing engine and most running gear with the two-seaters. The main differences, naturally, are in body styling and dimensions. Compared with the Bertone-styled car, the Mondial 8 rides a 91.4mm (3.6-inch) longer wheelbase (2642mm/104 inches), is five inches higher and three inches wider. The result is a more spacious air to the interior and greater comfort for four, though the back seat is still best reserved

Page opposite: At first glance, the 308 GTS looks little different from its berlinetta counterpart—unless the targa-like roof is removed. Car at top is the European version. Below it is the 1979 U.S.-spec. edition. Note limited service access to mid-mounted V-8. This page, above, upper left, and left: The U.S. 308 GTBi. Features included Bosch CIS fuel injection, Connolly leather interior trim, and fat Michelin TRX tires for 1981. Below: The '79 European-trim 308 GTS displays its Dino 246GT-inspired styling.

for children. Unfortunately, the new model is one of the heavier Ferraris seen in recent years, which accounts for some early press criticism of the car's decidedly un-Ferrari-like acceleration. This is no surprise as the 3.0-liter quad-cam V-8 has lost a few horses to U.S. emissions tuning and, as in current 308s, is rated at a relatively low 205 bhp (SAE net) at 6600 rpm.

Even so, there's certainly nothing wrong with any car that combines luxury appointments with the levels of handling and roadholding long associated with the Ferrari name, and the

Mondial 8 does just that. It's certainly the most "powered" Ferrari yet. Besides air conditioning, standard amenities include an electrically operated remote-control driver's door mirror and radio antenna, power steering, and power brakes. Also provided is an electronic monitoring system that keeps tabs on fluid levels, status of headlamp and taillight bulbs, and whether doors are fully closed. The interior is swathed in genuine English Connolly hide, and the leather-wrapped steering wheel can be adjusted for both reach and rake. The only option is an electrically operated sunroof.

If there's one area where the Mondial 8 disappoints it's

This page, top and above: Although now a familiar sight to Americans, the 308 GTS hardly seems to have aged. Right: The sumptuous interior of the mid-engine Mondial 8 provides decent space for four. Page opposite: The Mondial 8 in its initial 1980 European form (above) and in 1982 fuel-injected U.S. trim (below).

probably appearance. This latest Pininfarina design, like Bertone's GT4, suffers from a wheelbase that looks too long in relation to roof length, one penalty of trying to provide +2 seating in a mid-engine chassis. The front end recalls the Berlinetta Boxer, and carries an unobtrusive lip spoiler under an eggcrate grille mounted below a deep, black-rubber bumper. Headlamps pop up from the nose when needed, and there are auxiliary driving lamps recessed slightly in the bumper's face. But this nice introduction is spoiled by somewhat clumsy rear-quarter details, especially the large, black ducts on the bodysides and curious black strips on the trailing edges of the flying

Above: Not considered one of Pininfarina's design triumphs, the Mondial 8 (1982 U.S. version shown) nevertheless manages to look aggressively purposeful in this view. Left: Like the two-seat 308 GTB/GTS, Mondial 8 mounts Ferrari's 205-bhp (U.S.) V-8 transversely amidships. Here's the complete power pack ready for installation.

exercise much greater control over Ferrari production, even though Ferrari has been part of the Fiat empire since 1969. The happy result is that the Mondial 8 (as well as the newer 308s) are put together far better than earlier models. That bodes well for reliability, even for the sort of daily commuting and shopping chores to which most Ferrari owners would never dream of subjecting their cars. The Mondial 8 certainly has everything expected of a high-performance Italian supercar. While its commercial success remains to be seen, the mere fact it wears the Ferrari badge would seem to ensure its future.

buttress rear roof pillars. Like its predecessor, the Mondial 8 is chunky, but it's a busier and arguably less unified shape.

None of this, however, should spoil the appeal of Ferrari's latest four-place GT, which stands to be the most solidly built car ever to carry the prancing horse emblem. Since about 1980 Fiat has come to

THE FLAT-12 SPORTS/RACING CARS

Clay Reggazoni pilots the ground-hugging 312 PB

By the mid-'60s, Ferrari was well-known for its smooth and powerful V-12s. But there would also be 12-cylinder powerplants with the "flat" or horizontally opposed configuration in which the cylinder banks are situated 180 degrees from each other. This layout, which the Germans call "boxer," had been popularized by Porsche, among others, in the mass market, but it would be left to Ferrari to apply it to expensive racing and road machines. The first flat 12 Ferrari was the 1.5-liter 512 Formula 1 car, sometimes referred to as the 1512 F1, which Lorenzo Bandini drove in time trials for the 1964 Monza Grand Prix. However, the flat 12 engine would not be seriously used in F1 competition until 1970.

Developed from this car was the Sport 2000, first tested at Modena in 1968. Later called the 212 E Montagna, it had been devised by engineer Jacoponi for only one purpose: to win the European Hill Climb Championship, a crown Ferrari had captured on two previous occasions. Initially, power output was 290 bhp at a screaming 11,800 rpm. For the 1969 championship, power was increased to 315-320 bhp. Displacement was 1991cc/121.5 cid (65 x 50mm/2.56 x 1.97) with twin overhead camshafts for each cylinder bank, single plug per cylinder, and Lucas fuel injection. The five-speed gearbox sat behind the mid-mounted engine. The chassis (No. 0842) is believed to be that of the 206 SP spyder in which Gunter Klass was killed during practice at Mugello in July 1967. Peter Schetty drove the Sport 2000 in all seven events it entered, and won them all. Ferrari sat out the final round because these wins had given it the hillclimb crown, which had been a Porsche possession for years.

Meanwhile, there was another rule change affecting prototype

Right: Jackie Ickx takes the lead in the early stages of the BOAC 1000 at England's Brands Hatch circuit in 1971.

sports cars in international endurance racing. The FIA decreed that, effective January 1, 1972, the capacity limit for this group would be 3.0 liters. Ferrari was ready. At his December 1970 press conference, Enzo displayed the small, compact, beautifully designed 312 PB (Prototipo Boxer). In January 1971 he sent two of these cars to Argentina for the Buenos Aires 1000km, but only one made the grid, to be driven by Giunti and Arturo Merzario. The opposition was formidable, most of it coming from the big Porsche 917s. On lap 37, tragedy struck. Jean-Pierre Beltoise, in the Matra MS 600, ran out of fuel while coming out of the hairpin before the pits. Rather stupidly, he started pushing his

car across the track towards the pits, putting him right in the path of oncoming traffic. Mike Parkes in a Ferrari 512 avoided him, but Giunti couldn't. Smashing right into the Matra, his 312 PB exploded and burst into flames. Giunti was killed.

During the rest of the season the 312 PB often won the pole and frequently led races, but it was usually a DNF. But 1971 was more or less a development year for the car, and 1972 would be different. Ferrari prepared six 312 PBs, three for each race and three back-up cars, in an all-out effort to win the World Championship for Makes against the Matras and the new Alfa Romeo T33s. As it happened, the 312 PB won every race it entered (except Le Mans, which the French Matras won in a blitz of patriotic fervor). Ferrari team manager Peter Schetty had a

traumatic season as his drivers took little or no notice of his instructions or pit signals, and seemed to be competing more against each other than the other teams.

Displacement for the 312 PB was 2991cc/182.5 cid (80 x 49.6mm/3.15 x 1.95 inches). A five-speed gearbox was mounted aft of the amidships quad-cam engine, which ran on an 11.5:1 compression ratio and had Lucas fuel injection. Rated power was a musuclar 450 bhp at 11,000 rpm. The 312 PB went through various minor modifications during the 1972 season, including some detail body revisions. The team cars suffered numerous problems during the 1973 campaign, and despite running changes did not achieve the reliability of the Matras, losing the championship by 9 points. In all, approximately 10 chassis were built.

Below: A procession of 312Bs at the 1972 Daytona 6 Hours. Ronnie Peterson in car 6 placed 2nd overall. Car 4 with Reggazoni/Redman took 4th.

THE FLAT~12
GRAN TURISMOS

A GT-class 512 BB heads into the dusk at Le Mans.

Ferrari's first—and perhaps last—flat-12 road car, the 365 GT4 BB stands as perhaps the ultimate in gran turismo design. Big 5.0-liter "pancake" engine and low-slung Pininfarina styling combine to yield a top speed comfortably in excess of 160 mph. Design features include one-piece engine cover and single windshield wiper.

The 1972 Turin show saw a dazzling new Pininfarina design study destined to become Ferrari's first flat-12 road car. Production did not begin until 1973 for the 365 GT4BB, the type designation meaning gran turismo, 4-cam berlinetta boxer.

The 4930cc (300.8-cid) "pancake" powerplant was installed directly behind the snug two-seat cockpit and ahead of the rear axle centerline. Drive was taken to the rear wheels through a five-speed all-synchromesh gearbox and single dry-plate clutch.

Suspension employed the geometry expected in Italian supercars by this time: unequal-length A-arms, coil springs, and telescopic shocks all-around. Steel was used for the hulking, low-slung body except for hood, doors, and engine cover

(aluminum) and the lower body panels (fiberglass and painted matte-black regardless of body color). The prototype's frame was built up of round- and oval-section steel tubing, but this was switched to square and rectangular section on production models for easier assembly, which was carried out as usual by Scaglietti.

Though its styling was unmistakably Pininfarina, the BB looked like something from the future and more like a race-ready Group 5 prototype than a car you could actually drive on public roads. Body panels appeared to be sculpted to "melt" around major mechanical components, particularly the long hood that dipped low to meet the pavement. Despite its very masculine shape, styling was rounder and more flowing than the Daytona's, helped by the BB's greater overall length. Like the Daytona, it wore beautiful five-spoke alloy wheels, with knock-off center hubs on European cars.

The slinky body put the BB's driving position low to the ground

191

Ferraris aren't usually thought of as drag race champs, but the Berlinetta Boxer with its lightning acceleration could be. Here, an early 365 GT4 BB is tested in Sweden.

and more toward the front wheels than the back ones. The cockpit was comfortable, provided you weren't too tall. There wasn't much luggage space, a common complaint about mid-engine cars, but then the BB wasn't made for hauling cargo, just hauling. *Road & Track* magazine's 1975 road test yielded a quarter-mile time of 15.5 seconds at a terminal speed of 102.5 mph. That was performance comparable to a '60s muscle car, and in a way the BB was a sort of Italian muscle car. It certainly had the same kind of heft, tipping the scales at a weighty 3420 pounds. There were also complaints about the car's high-effort controls, particularly the stiff clutch and the gated

shifter, both of which demanded a good deal of driver skill for smooth progress. Like the Daytona, the BB suffered from heavy steering at lower speeds, something of a surprise considering its mid-engine layout, but it was perfect at the higher velocities this car could achieve. Under good conditions, a BB would see the far side of 160 mph, with perhaps a bit more to come.

A modified version of the BB was displayed at the 1976 Paris Salon wearing the simpler 512 BB designation. The engine was bored and stroked a bit to bring displacement up to 4942cc (301.6 cid). The four triple-choke Weber carbs of the previous model were retained, but although rated power was down from 380 to 360 bhp (DIN), it was developed at a less frantic 6200 rpm instead of 7000. Appearance alterations

were few. Distinguishing points were NACA-type air intakes on the lower bodysides ahead of the rear wheels, a shallow lip spoiler under the nose, and four taillights instead of six.

In an early-1982 comparison test between the 512 BB and its nearest rival, the wild-looking Lamborghini Countach, *Road & Track* reported the Ferrari's 0-60 mph time at 5.1 seconds and clocked a 13.5-second quarter-mile at 100.5 mph. Top speed was a blistering 168 mph. And that was for a car detoxed to meet U.S. emissions standards! Corresponding figures for the Lambo were 5.7 seconds, 14.1 seconds at 104 mph, and 150 mph. Noted race driver Sam Posey did the testing, and summed up the Boxer as a car time had left

continued on page 209

365 P2/3

The 365 P2/3 debuted in 1965, and was raced by both factory-sponsored and private teams. It was very competitive yet relatively simple to maintain.

330 P4

The final development of the
330P series, the 330 P4 had an
entirely new engine, designed by
Rocchi, with three valves per
cylinder (two intake and one
exhaust). One of the three P4s
built is shown here. Owned by
David Clarke, it was routinely
raced for several years, but has
now been retired to be lovingly
preserved.

195

512M

The 512M was a modification of the factory's 512S built to compete in the 1968 Sports Car Championship. The S was too heavy and thus not competitive, hence the changes to its body-work and mechanicals. The 512M was campaigned by the factory and privateers, but did not enjoy a great deal of success.

Dino 206SP

Derived from the Dino 166P of 1965 was this mid-engine 206SP, one of the most beautiful of racing machines. However, its track record didn't match its appearance. Only a few were built as the Ferrari factory was experiencing labor troubles at the time and was also heavily engaged in its Formula I progam.

Dino 246GT

From the 206SP and the 206GT came the Dino 246GT, the least expensive Ferrari ever built. Its V-6 engine was mounted transversely behind the cockpit, and was made by Fiat. It was also used in the Lancia Stratos rally car and the Fiat Dino. Some 4000 of the 246GTs were built between 1969 and 1973.

512 Berlinetta
Boxer

To many, the 512BB is the ultimate in high-performance automobiles. Its power unit is similar to that of the flat-12 once used in Ferrari's Formula I racing cars. The example shown here is owned by Chuck Jordan, Director of Design for General Motors, long a Ferrari admirer.

512 Berlinetta
Boxer

The 512BB replaced the 365GT/4 Berlinetta Boxer in 1976. The newer model is distinguished only by a modest "chin" spoiler and four taillamps instead of six. Initially, the BB had a carbureted 4.4-liter flat-12. The 512 has a 5.0-liter enlargement of this engine, with electronic fuel injection from 1981.

308 GTB

Ferrari's first V-8 touring car arrived in 1973, the mid-engine 308GT4 2+2 styled by Bertone. This was followed in 1975 by the two-seat 308GTB, with flowing lines reminiscent of the Dino 246GT. A spyder version, more properly considered a "targa", appeared two years later. The latest 308s have electronic fuel injection.

308 GTSi

The 308GTSi shows a style and grace unmatched by any other car in its class. Critics already consider it and the 308GTBi future "classics."

behind: "You know, I can't avoid the idea that Ferrari has outgrown the desire to make a car like the Boxer. This was once the bread and butter of the company, but that was at a different time.... Now, they have become super technical...and while the Boxer might be exotic in looks and exclusivity, it certainly doesn't take advantage of the latest automotive technology."

Posey was probably right. By the dawn of the '80s, cars like the Boxer were almost anti-social, even among very well-heeled customers like Ferrari's. There were few places (other than a race track, that is) where you could really drive it at the speeds it was designed for, so there was little reason for owning one, except perhaps for its magnificent styling and engineering. Sad to say, the world had changed, and

Right: The flat-12 Ferrari engine, a magnificent example of the art of metal casting. Below: The 1982 version of the 512 BB, now designated 512 BBi to denote its standard Bosch fuel injection. Note unusual "airfoil" over rear window.

single-purpose machines like the Boxer no longer had much of a place in it. Even Maranello came to recognize this. At this writing, there is nothing known to be on the drawing boards as a direct replacement for the BB. Also unknown is how long this magnificent flyer will remain in production. But one thing is certain: the Boxer's passing will mark the end of an era for Ferrari, and the world will be a little poorer for the loss of this exciting car.

Although Ferrari's racing activities have been restricted to Formula 1 for the past several years, the 512 BB has represented the marque in sports car competition. With factory

support, a number of independents and two Ferrari distributors, the Chinetti NART organization and the Pozzi concern in Paris, have campaigned BBs, notably in the 24 Hours of Le Mans. The car's best finish came in 1982 when Ron and Patti Spengler's Prancing Horse Racing BB (chassis no. 34445 LM) ran 322 laps at an average speed of 182.824 kph (113.602 mph), good for 6th overall and 3rd in class. It was a very creditable showing against the factory-backed Porsches.

The shape of Ferraris to come may very well lie in an innovative show car called the Pinin. Making its world premiere at the 1980 Turin exposition, this clean-lined four-door sedan was named in honor of Battista Pininfarina, founder of the design firm that bears his name and which celebrated its 50th anniversary that year. Considering its long, close, and historic association with Maranello, it was only

natural the *carrozzeria* should design this commemorative showpiece around Ferrari mechanicals. Most of these are familiar. Suspension and transmission are borrowed from the 400, the engine from the 512

BB. The reason design director Leonardo Fioravanti chose the Ferrari flat-12 instead of its V-12 or V-8 was to achieve a low hoodline for good aerodynamics. (Incidentally, Fioravanti is the man who has supervised design of

Looking like a race car even in street trim, the 512 BB becomes positively wild when outfitted for the track. These examples prepared for Le Mans sport tall tail-mounted spoilers and massively flared wheel arches to accommodate racing rubber.

Above and page opposite: The 512 BB of England's Rosso Racing on the track and being prepared. Though not official factory entries, a number of 512s have represented Ferrari in international GT endurance racing in recent years. Right: A special turbocharged 512 BB awaits final preparation in France in June 1977.

all the Pininfarina Ferraris since the Dino 206 with the exception of the 365 GTC/4.)

The Pinin's appearance is strikingly handsome in its simplicity, a sharp contrast with the complexity of its equipment. Among its exterior innovations are the new "homofocal" rectangular headlamp (by Lucas), a new type of taillight lens (by Carello) that can be matched to any paint color, and flush-fit door glass that overlaps the roof pillars, again to minimize air turbulence. There is an apparent absence of bumpers on the Pinin, but they are there: you just can't see them, so skillfully do they blend into the body contours. The slightly pointed front end is

dominated by a wide eggcrate grille echoing Ferraris of the early '50s. This is a large car by today's standards (108.1-inch wheelbase and 189.8-inch overall length), yet it manages to look fleet and graceful, powerful yet

elegant. Its full wheel cutouts and five-spoke alloy wheels (with inward curving spokes to duct air to the disc brakes) lend an aura of purposefulness and speed that belies the size.

Inside, the Pinin combines the

latest in electronics with the ultimate in luxury. A central console runs the full length of the cabin, making this strictly a four-seater. Each seat is a specially designed bucket covered in genuine Connolly leather, which also runs along the doors and instrument panel. The driver's station features analog electronic instrumentation directly ahead of a small, thickly padded, leather-rim steering wheel. The console's front portion houses such space-age accoutrements as a travel computer, maintenance reminder system, and mechanical troubleshooting system. Another console overhead puts switches for the power seats close at hand, along with reading lamps. Rear-seat passengers are well-catered for, too. They have their own travel computer (with LED readouts on the overhead console), plus headphones for private radio listening and even a telephone, all contained in a pod on the driveshaft tunnel.

For a show car, the Pinin was

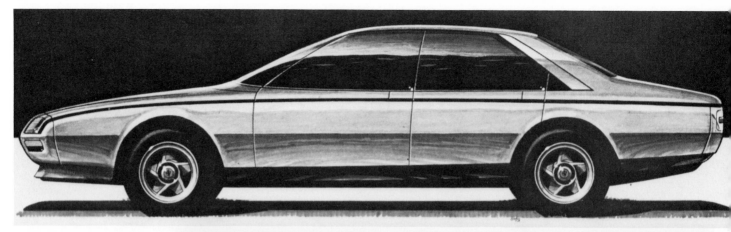

This page and page opposite: The futuristic Pinin show car as shown in the official Pininfarina brochure issued shortly before the car itself (shown at right) was displayed in 1980. Powered by the compact Ferrari flat-12, chosen to achieve a low, aerodynamically efficient hoodline, the Pinin bristles with the latest in electronics, and incorporates several new body design features. The Pinin is strongly rumored to be the next production Ferrari.

remarkably well-finished inside and out, and quite practical. Indeed, most observers at Turin noted the design could be readily adapted for small-scale production within the limits of existing technology. Enzo Ferrari himself liked the car so much that he suggested Pininfarina do just that. At this writing, it appears you'll be able to buy this car or something very close to it by the mid-'80s. Despite its size and that thirsty 12-cylinder engine, it would almost certainly find a ready market even at a price that would very likely be over $100,000. The road-ready Pinin might even retain the race-bred flat-12. It would surely emerge with the flush glass, "invisible" taillights, and all the other styling features that give the show car its air of timeless grace.

214

If nothing else, the existence of the Pinin and the good prospects for its production show that a new Ferrari model is still very much a dream car. Virtually every car to bear the sign of the defiant prancing horse has been a car to inspire visions of blasting down the *autostrada* at an easy 120 mph; of winding your way through Alpine passes to the music of a thoroughbred engine; of pulling up to the swankiest night spot in town while basking in the admiring glances from envious onlookers. A Ferrari is all this and more. It's a tradition, a colorful legacy of engineering excellence forged in the heat of competition, tempered by the drive and genius of a handful of legendary pioneers. Happily, it's a tradition that seems certain to endure for many years to come.

THE NOTABLE GRAND PRIX CARS

After World War II only three marques were realistically able to field a team of grand prix cars right away. One was Alfa Romeo, which had been developing its Type 158, a 1.5-liter supercharged straight-eight car, before Italy entered the war. Another was Talbot-Lago (or, as some prefer it, Lago-Talbot) which had a 4.5-liter unsupercharged car. The third was Maserati. Mercedes-Benz and Auto Union also could have put up teams, but they were banned from racing for an unspecified period after 1945 for obvious

reasons. There were also the small-displacement *voiturettes* from Britain such as the E.R.A. and Alta (the latter's four-cylinder engine also powered the HWM that later harried the 1.5 supercharged Ferrari V-12s in some races). Delahaye in France could also have fielded some unsupercharged cars.

Barely three weeks after V-J day, the French, reflecting their love of motor racing, organized a meeting in the *Bois du Boulogne* area of Paris of all places. The event was the *Coupe des Prisonniers* run over a 43-lap,

75-mile course. The race was so short because, after all, fuel and tires were in very short supply. Minimum displacement was 3.0 liters. Wimille won in a supercharged Bugatti 4.7, and a single-seat Talbot-Lago with Raymond Sommer at the wheel was 2nd. Talbot was also represented by a variety of its prewar 4.0- and 4.5-liter sports cars and a 1939 offset-engine grand prix car. The monoposto Talbot-Lago (a number of which were later built and raced successfully) was a very handsome machine.

Enzo Ferrari was no doubt watching such early postwar meets, itching to get back to constructing his own cars. Although he had not yet created the first car bearing his name, he had already designed and constructed several racers. These included the two twin-engine *Bi-Motore* Alfa Romeos, with Luigi Bazzi, and, with help from Gioacchini Colombo, the supercharged 1500cc Alfetta (subsequently the Type 158/159 that was a pain in Enzo Ferrari's neck until it left the scene at the end of the 1952 season). Just

before Italy entered the war, he had also built the 815 from Fiat parts, and two of these had run in the 1940 Mille Miglia. So with all his expertise, Ferrari was about to re-enter the racing game. He had his new Maranello factory, even though it had suffered slight bomb damage, and sufficient cash from his war contract work. Most importantly, he knew everyone worth knowing, and still employed a number of technicians who had been with him in prewar days.

Ferrari had his heart set on

racing a V-12 engine, mainly for personal reasons, including his love for "the song of the twelve." Thus it was no surprise he would ask Colombo, who had been involved with the prewar V-12 racing Alfas, to be his chief engineer. Colombo had been with Alfa Romeo since January 1924, and had worked as a draftsman with Vittorio Jano. When Jano was eased out in 1937, Colombo naturally expected to replace him. Instead he was passed over in favor of Wilfredo Ricart, a Fascist follower. So, Colombo eagerly

Jacky Ickx hits a bumpy patch in the 312 B2 during the 1972-73 season.

Above: Peter Whitehead's 125 F1 car is shown here fully restored in this 1973 photograph taken at the entrance to the Donington Park Circuit in England.

accepted Ferrari's invitation.

Work began on the new V-12 in 1946. The idea was to have three GP cars ready for the following year. However, it was a sports version that raced first. The grand prix machine wasn't completed until September 1948, in time for the Italian Grand Prix at Valentino Park. Giuseppe Farina, Raymond Sommer, and Prince Bira did the driving. Sommer took 3rd while Bira suffered transmission failure and Farina stuffed his car into some straw bales. As might be expected, this Type 125 had its problems but, with a brilliant engineering technician like Bazzi around, they were eventually ironed out. As a result, Colombo's V-12 and its derivations would power many racing Ferraris, up to and including the 512S and M competition sports cars of 1970-71.

Because this powerplant was the heart of so many Ferraris, especially the early road cars, its original design is worth examination. The cylinder banks were set at a relatively narrow 60-degree angle. Bore and stroke were 55 x 52.5mm (2.17 x 2.07 inches) for displacement of

1497mm (91.4 cid). The block, crankcase, and detachable cylinder heads were cast in aluminum alloy. Wet cylinder liners were shrunk in, and the cylinder heads held them in compression against the block. A ridge two-thirds of the way down the liners allowed for a metal-to-metal join with the block. Each cylinder bank had a single overhead camshaft running in six bearings and chain-driven from the front of the seven-main-bearing crankshaft. Valves were opened by means of rocker arms and closed by two hairpin springs each. Both intake and exhaust valves were inclined at an included angle of 60 degrees, giving more or less hemispherical combustion chambers. A Weber 40 DO3C carburetor was situated in the vee with a single-stage Roots-type supercharger at the front running at 1.22 times crankshaft speed. Twin magnetos driven from the rear of the camshafts sparked one plug per cylinder. On a compression ratio of 6.5:1, this engine developed 225 bhp peak power at 7000 rpm. By contrast, the Alfa 158 had 310 bhp at its disposal. To compensate for the power difference, the Ferrari needed a light, compact chassis.

The engine had to be built from scratch because material supplies

were short in those days. This also dictated a specially designed gearbox, which turned out to be five-speed non-synchromesh transmission mounted in unit with the engine. The gearshift was on the left of the cockpit and operated in an open gate. There was a single dry-plate clutch, and an open driveshaft ran to the rear-mounted final drive. The tubular chassis was composed of oval-section main members, a box-section front crossmember, and a welded tubular upper structure for the bodywork, which was formed from aluminum panels. The front suspension used unequal-length A-arms and a transverse leaf spring, while the rear employed swing-axle halfshafts, radius arms, and torsion bars. Houdaille vane-type shock absorbers took care of damping all round, and the hydraulic brakes had finned alloy drums. The 16-inch center-lock Borrani wire wheels were shod with Pirelli tires (front 5.50 x 16, rear 6.50 x 16). Wheelbase was no more than 2160mm (85 inches), with a 1255mm (49.4-inch) front track and 1200mm (47.2-inch) rear track. The Type 125 weighed a mere 700kg (1543 lbs) less fuel and driver.

In its final form for 1950 the Type 125 engine was substantially modified. This involved adoption of twin camshafts per cylinder bank, two-stage supercharging, and a Weber 50 WCF carburetor. Compression ratio was boosted to 7:1, which raised output to 315 bhp at 7500 rpm. The gearbox was now mounted at the rear in unit with a ZF limited-slip differential. The rear suspension was reworked with universal joints for the halfshafts and double parallel radius rods per side; a De Dion tube was carried in a slot on the differential housing, and a transversely mounted leaf spring was added. Owing to poor handling characteristics, the original wheelbase was lengthened to 2320mm (91.3 inches).

After the 1948 Italian Grand Prix, both the Ferrari and Alfa Romeo teams passed up the British GP at Silverstone in October in order to prepare for the Autodrome Grand Prix at Monza later the same month. Sommer was in a comfortable 2nd place behind Wimille's Alfa when he was overcome by an attack of asthma, forcing him out of the race after the 7th lap. Then Farina went out with transmission failure. The next race for the 125F1 was the minor Circuit of Garda over 183 miles on the track at Sala. Farina's car remained in one piece and won, beating a 2.0-liter Spyder Corsa Ferrari driven by Sterzi. The 1948 season ended with the Gran Premio Penya Rhin race held on the Pedralbes street course. Ferrari sent cars for Farina, Bira, and an unknown, Jose Pola. The first two retired, probably with transmission failure, while Pola blew his motor.

So, the year was hardly a success for Ferrari. The works retained one of these cars and sold one to Tony Vandervell, the thin-wall bearing king, who renamed it the Thin Wall Special. The third car was bought by British farmer Peter Whitehead, who raced it occasionally with the factory's blessing. But that winter, Ferrari signed up two of the best drivers around, Alberto Ascari and Luigi Villaresi, who

Above: Photographed at Boreham in England, 1952, a detail view of the 2.0-liter V-12 of the 166 Formula 2 car.

had been driving Maseratis for Scuderia Ambrosiana.

Alfa Romeo decided to withdraw from racing for a time at the end of 1948, feeling that the aging 158 could no longer match the Ferraris. Thus, 1949 turned out to be a Ferrari/Maserati duel. The 125F1 factory cars were delayed until the Belgian Grand Prix in June, when they placed 2nd (Villoresi), 3rd (Ascari), and 4th (Whitehead). They went on to win the Swiss, Dutch, Italian, and Czechoslovakian events (the last won by Whitehead as a private entry). All told, 1949 saw Ferraris score in 19 of the most important races. Counting the lesser events, the season total was 32 wins, 19 2nds, and 12 3rds.

Apart from Formula 1 there were *formule libre* and Formula 2 events staged in the early postwar years, and the 125's basic design proved useful for these series. Increasing bore and stroke to 60 x 58.8mm (2.36 x 2.31 inches) gave a displacement of 1995cc (121.7 cid) for the 166 Formule Libre model, fitted with one Weber 40 DORC carburetor and a single-stage supercharger that yielded 310 bhp at 7000 rpm. The Formula 2 car, designated 166F2, had the same displacement, no supercharger, and three Weber 32 DCF carburetors for 155 bhp at 7000 rpm. In 1949, it won every

race it entered, and won 13 of 15 races it contested in 1950.

For 1951, the 166F2 received a slight power increase (to 160 bhp). At the same time, the factory issued what seemed to be an interim Formula 1 contender, the 212 F1. It shared basic parts with the 166F2 but had a 68mm (2.68-inch) bore giving a displacement of 2562.2cc (156.4 cid). With three Weber 38 DCF carbs and a tight 13:1 compression it was rated at 200 bhp at 7500 rpm. During 1951, Swiss driver Rudi Fischer ran one as a Formula 2 car in grand prix events. This engine was also used successfully in Ferrari's Type 212 roadgoing sports models.

During 1947, Aurelio Lampredi came to Maranello from the Piaggio aircraft and scooter concern to be an assistant to Colombo. He was not a trained engineer, but like a number of people had an intuitive sense for things mechanical. He and Luigi Bazzi had the job of sorting out the problems which had affected the early racing cars. Lampredi was a man with definite ideas. For a short period, he quit Ferrari out of dissatisfaction with his relatively minor role. But, as noted earlier, he was persuaded to return when Enzo agreed to let him design and build a large-displacement unsupercharged engine, which Lampredi felt was the best answer for speed and reliability in grand prix. Colombo, however, was a proponent of supercharging, and as Enzo now seemed to be favoring Lampredi's view, he departed for Alfa Romeo to see whether he could extract more power from the 158/159.

Lampredi's new engine built on Colombo's work. The big difference was that its block and cylinder heads were four inches longer than in the earlier V-12 and its bore centers spaced 108mm (4.25 inches) apart instead of 90mm (3.54 inches). For this reason, it became known as the long-block. Lampredi was assigned to develop three versions: a 4.5-liter V-12 to challenge the Alfa 159, an inline four for the new 2.5-liter GP formula effective for 1954, and (because Ferrari correctly predicted the 1952-53 World Championship would be based on Formula 2) a 2.0-liter four.

As a test bed for the large-capacity V-12, the 275F1 was built in 1950 with a 3.3-liter (201.4-cid) 60-degree engine. Ascari drove it at Spa-Francorchamps in the Belgian Grand Prix, and while it proved reliable it was painfully slow. It did, however, finish 5th. Its next race should have been the French Grand Prix at Rheims, but it was so slow in practice it was withdrawn. A successor, the 4.1-liter (250.2-cid) 340F1, was ready for the *Grand Prix des Nations,* to be run over a street circuit at Geneva in July. This car, intended as a prototype of the 4.5-liter machine, had a new chassis formed by two parallel rectangular-section side members, with a plate at the front to locate the front suspension. A tubular crossmember at the rear of the clutch housing and another one behind the halfshafts completed the assembly, to which the body was welded.

The 340F1 was driven at Geneva by Ascari, while Villoresi

had the 275F1. They faced the full might of Alfa Romeo, with Fangio, Farina, Taruffi, and De Graffenried all driving Type 158s. In qualifying runs Ascari and Villoresi were nearly as fast as Fangio, who took the pole. But in the race Fangio built up a 30-second lead over Ascari. Seven laps from the end of the 68-lap dash Villoresi found an oil patch and crashed into a spectator area, killing several people (he was thrown out onto the road, and the car was a total wreck). Farina tried to take avoiding action, and in doing so crashed into the hay bales. Ascari parked his Ferrari with a blown engine.

For the Italian event at Monza in September two of the new 375F1 cars appeared for Ascari and test driver Dorino Serafini (Villoresi was still recovering from his accident). These 4.5-liter (274.6-cid) engines developed 330 bhp at 6500 rpm, and used the larger 40 DCF Weber carburetors, but were otherwise much like the 340s. Farina and Fangio had the updated Alfa 158, now designated Type 159. Ascari led the race at one stage, but blew his engine on lap 22. When Serafini came in to change tires, he took that car and worked it up from 6th to 2nd, where he remained until crossing the finish line nearly one and a half minutes behind Farina. Ferrari was now a serious

challenger to Alfa Romeo's supremacy in Formula 1. The Alfa team missed the Spanish Grand Prix, but Ferrari entered three cars: 375s for Ascari and Serafini, a 340F1 for Taruffi. The opposition was not formidable, but the Ferraris showed their reliability by taking the top three places. Ascari was 1st at a race-average 93.93 mph.

Villoresi started the 1951 season in great style by winning at Syracuse and Pau with the 375F1. Meantime, the factory was trying to extract more power from the 4.5 engine. The 159 Alfa was now producing 405 bhp at 10,500 rpm, but its 1.5-liter supercharged straight eight guzzled fuel at an alarming rate: 1.5 mpg against the 7-8 mpg of the Ferraris. Maranello still had an important time advantage in needing fewer pit stops. For the San Remo GP in April the 375F1 got two plugs per cylinder and redesigned cylinder heads. The second set of plugs was placed outboard of the vee, which necessitated modifications to the water passages and exhaust manifolds. Brakes were also improved for better cooling. Ascari, as team leader, had the revised car, and won handily at 64.03 mph over 90 laps of the twisting 2.1-mile course.

The Alfa and Ferrari teams had been "missing" each other all

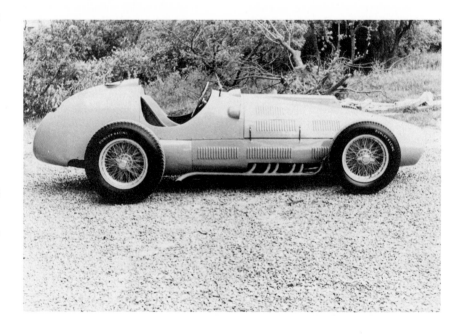

season until the Swiss event at Bremgarten in May. All the 375F1s had the new brakes, but only Ascari and Taruffi had 24-plug engines; Villoresi had the older unit. It was not a good race for Team Ferrari as Ascari was still suffering a badly burned arm from a Formula 2 race, and was off form. Villoresi was blinded by spray from the torrential rain that fell during the race, and ran off the road. This left Piero Taruffi to uphold the honor of the prancing horse. In a display of brilliant driving he passed Farina three laps from the finish to take 2nd behind Fangio's Alfa. The Belgian and French Grands Prix fell to Alfa, with Ferrari settling for 2nd and 3rd places. But the tables turned in the British and German events. In the meantime, the Ferraris went to Pescara, where Froilan Gonzales won.

The next Alfa/Ferrari confrontation was at Bari in September. The race was Alfa's, but Gonzales was having a good season and finished 2nd. Still, Ferrari was trailing. Alfa was favored to take the Italian Grand Prix because it had an improved car ready, the 159M (M for Maggiorata). Fangio, Farina, and Bonetto would each drive one, while De Graffenried had an older 159. Ferrari entered five 375s. Ascari, Villoresi, and Gonzales got the 24-plug engine in a revised body with a higher cowl incorporating a built-in perspex windshield and a modified tail incorporating a headrest. Taruffi drove the normal 24-plug car, and Chico Landi piloted a 1950 12-plug 375. It is interesting to note that in qualifying Landi drove the prototype 2.5-liter four-cylinder 625 F1 destined for the 1954 season. The Ferraris made a meal of the Alfas, taking 1st, 2nd, 4th, and 5th places. Farina, who should have been black-flagged for a leaking fuel tank, was 3rd.

Ferrari had won the last three championship events, and if it hadn't been for a tactical error would have won the last race at Barcelona in October. It was decided to use 16-inch-diameter wheels for this race whereas Ferraris had run mainly on 17-inch rims all year. All four team drivers suffered tread separation. Fangio took 1st for Alfa, but Gonzales got past Farina to finish 2nd. Fangio thus won the World Drivers' Championship with 31 points, trailed by Ascari (25 points) and Gonzales (24 points).

Alfa Romeo hoped to produce a new car for 1952, but the Italian government failed to come up with the expected subsidy. At least the marque went out as a winner in its duel with Ferrari.

Ferrari had no strong competition in 1952 from Maserati, Talbot, Simca, or BRM, so some of the 375 F1s were sold. One car was prepared for Ascari to drive in the Indianapolis 500, and three others went to Howard Keck, Johnny Mauro, and the Grant Piston Ring company for the Memorial Day event. The Grant car was qualified by Johnny Pearson, the 1950 Indy winner, but he decided to drive his Offenhauser car instead. Mauro failed to qualify. Bill Vukovitch qualified Howard Keck's car as well as the American Fuel Injection Engineering Special, which qualified with a higher speed, so that's the car he ran. Ascari qualified his 375 at 134.308 mph (25th fastest). Lying 12th during the race, the car suffered a locked hub that caused a spin and a collapsed rear wheel.

The Formula 2 V-12s had made only sporadic appearances in 1951 since the factory was concentrating on the 375 for Formula 1, but they did well as in the two previous years. Lampredi was concentrating on the 2.0- and 2.5-liter four-cylinder engines for the 500 F2 and the 625 F1. The 2.0-liter's first contest was the Modena Grand Prix in September, but it was retired by Villoresi. The V-12 formula cars continued to be raced by independents such as Scuderia Marzotto and Ecurie Espadon (run by Rudi Fischer).

The 500 F2 had a 90 x 78mm (3.54 x 3.07-inch) bore and stroke, aluminum alloy crankcase cast *en bloc*, and a detachable cylinder head with screw-in liners. The crankshaft used five main bearings. Twin overhead camshafts were gear-driven. There were twin magnetos driven from the rear of the camshaft and sparking two plugs per cylinder. With two Weber 50 DCO carburetors and a compression ratio of 11.5:1, this power unit was rated at 165 bhp at 7000 rpm. A four-branch manifold fed

Page opposite: The Type 375 from the early '50s with bodywork as used at the Indianapolis 500. This page: The 500 F2 with Mike Hawthorn the likely driver here.

exhaust gases into a single pipe. A four-speed non-synchro gearbox was mounted at the back with a ZF limited-slip differential. Chassis design and suspension layout followed the 375 F1, although scaled down. Wheelbase was 2160mm (85 inches).

Over two years of production the 500 F2 saw only minor modifications. In early 1952, four Weber 45 DOE carburetors were fitted and there was a switch to four stub exhausts, both of which raised power to 170 bhp. Later that year the two magnetos were mounted at the front of the engine. For 1953, two Weber 50 DCOA carburetors were used and two twin-branch exhaust manifolds, leading into a single large-diameter pipe, were adopted.

The 500 F2 could well be the winningest race car in history, capturing no less than 14 world championship events in succession in 1952-53. In 33 races it was bested on only three occasions, at Rheims in 1952 by a Gordini (Jean Behra) and at Syracuse and Monza in 1953 by Maserati (Emmanuel de Graffenried and Juan Manuel Fangio, respectively). Ferrari, of course, won the Manufacturers' World Championship and Alberto

Below: The 625 F1 car as driven by Maurice Trintignant. This model's only big win came at the 1954 Buenos Aires GP.

Ascari the World Drivers' Championship in both years.

This win streak should have extended into 1954. The new 2.5-liter 625 F1 four-cylinder car had proved reliable, and drivers liked its handling. However, Ferrari's plans were upset by Mercedes, which would return to racing once more, and the Maseratis, which were fast if not always reliable.

During 1953, another new Ferrari was being developed, the Type 553. Two ran at Monza in that year's Italian Grand Prix, driven by Umberto Maglioli and Piero Carini. The latter retired, though, and the former could do no better than 8th. In its earliest form, the 553's 2.0-liter engine had a bore and stroke of 93 x 73.5mm (3.66 x 2.89 inches). Both were stretched to 100 x 79.5mm (3.94 x 3.13) for 2497cc (152.4 cid) to conform to the new 1954 specifications. Although its engine was developed from Lampredi's four, the rest of the 553 was completely new. It was known as the Squalo because of its shark-like appearance resulting from side-mounted fuel tanks. Though squat and aggressive-looking, the car didn't live up to its looks in performance. Its best showing came in the 1954 Spanish Grand Prix, which Mike Hawthorn won at an average speed of 97.17 mph.

Usually, the 553 engine was

raced in a 625 F1 chassis, which handled a lot better than the Squalo's. But the factory would rather forget 1954 and 1955, because the 625 F1 lacked power and was not competitive. Apart from Maurice Trintignant's private entry at the Buenos Aires race, which he won, the story was mostly minor placings. The 553 was available by July 1954, but failed to make any impression. For the rest of the season its engine powered the 625 F1, but without the desired results. The 555 F1, also known as the Supersqualo, appeared in 1955 but was no improvement. Ferrari was now without a fast or reliable car for 1956. There was nothing to replace the 625, 553 or 555 except for a 1.5-liter V-6 machine that wouldn't be raceworthy for a while. But help was on the way.

When Vittorio Jano left Alfa Romeo in the late '30s, he moved to Lancia. There he engineered some interesting cars, including some competitive sports/racing cars. Lancia wanted very much to join the ranks of grand prix contenders, and to this end Jano had come up with a 2.5-liter V-8 machine, the D50. This had a number of novel features, such as two pontoons on outriggers between the front and rear wheels. These were fuel tanks, but also had separate sections for the oil supply. It was also a light car. Holes were drilled wherever feasible to keep weight down without weakening the car structurally. After many teething troubles, the D50 arrived at the Spanish Grand Prix towards the end of the 1954 season. There were cars for Alberto Ascari and Luigi Villoresi, who had terminated their contracts with Ferrari, wanting to drive winners not losers. Ascari led the race early until clutch problems led to his retirement on lap 10. He had, however, run the fastest lap, 100.80 mph. Villoresi didn't last as long, going out at the end of lap 2 with broken brakes.

By May 1955, Lancia was in dire financial trouble, unable to pursue the D50's development because the government was

unwilling to give any more help. The Italian Automobile Club, feeling the Lancias had potential and aware of Ferrari's plight, had all the D50s and their equipment handed over to him. Jano also came with the package, so Ferrari and Jano were together again. Under Enzo's direction the cars ran in a few minor events and three major grands prix in 1955 with further development in mind. Over the winter of 1955-56 this work went ahead. The Lancia body was redesigned by integrating pontoons with the main structure, and Ferrari signed world champion Fangio (Ascari was killed in 1955 while testing a Ferrari sports car at Monza).

The Ferrari/Lancias didn't do spectacularly in 1956, but Fangio scored enough points to retain his world drivers' crown. However, he left at the end of the season, disgruntled at not always getting the best cars and at Enzo's aloofness from team drivers. After another depressing year in 1957, the Ferrari/Lancia was finished. Besides, Enzo was now more interested in Jano's new 1.5-liter 65-degree V-6 for 1958 Formula 2.

This car, the 156 F2, showed definite promise in 1957 when it placed twice, a 3rd at Naples for Musso and a 1st at Rheims for Trintignant. Ferrari wasn't at all enthusiastic about Formula 2, but this car was important to him as a test bed for the Dino 246 F1 (2.4-liter 65-degree V-6), which would be his GP weapon for 1958. Between 1957 and 1960 there were nine variations (mostly minor) of the Dino 246 F1, including a Dino 256 F1.

Even though 1958 was an exciting year and a reasonably successful one, it was overshadowed by tragedy. Mike Hawthorn became World Drivers Champion. His only outright win was the French Grand Prix, but he accumulated sufficient points in other events to take the title with the Dino 246 F1. He then retired from racing, only to die in a road accident in England in January 1959. At Rheims, the fast and flambouyant Musso took

a right-hander too fast, and ran off onto the grass. The car rolled, and he was thrown out. In the German Grand Prix at the Nurburgring, Peter Collins took the Pflangarten right-hander very fast, hit the bank, and rolled his car over the hedge. He was killed. With all this, 1958 was not a year to remember with any pleasure.

By 1960, the Dino 246 F1 was looking quite dated next to the British lightweight rear-engine machines. But it had a final fling in that year's Italian Grand Prix on the banked road course at Monza. The British stayed away as they decided the banking would be too rough for their cars' suspensions. The Dino 246 F1 ended its competition service in fine fashion, with Phil Hill and Richie Ginther 1st and 2nd and Belgian Willy Mairesse 3rd.

Enzo Ferrari was now ready to follow the rear-engine trend in Formula car design, and confirmed this by sending a prototype to Monaco equipped with the 2.4-liter Dino V-6. Ginther had the drive, but the car was not competitive and retired with final drive failure. Also in 1960, the factory had a new 1.5-liter V-6 car, the Dino 156 F2. Running in July at the Solitude Ring in West Germany, Von Trips won easily, and broke the lap record in the process. Ferrari missed that year's U.S. Grand Prix at Riverside as Enzo deemed the whole winter would be needed to prepare for 1961. There were to be two versions of the 156 F1, one

with a 65-degree 1.5 V-6 and one with similar displacement but with a 120-degree V-6. Both engines had 73mm (2.87-inch) bores but the 65-degree unit had a stroke of 59.1mm (2.33), the 120-degree 58.8mm (2.31).

The winter's preparation certainly paid off. Phil Hill won the Belgian and Italian Grands Prix with the 120 V-6, and scored enough points elsewhere to become the first American to win a world drivers title. At the same time, the young Italian Giancarlo Baghetti won at Syracuse, Naples, and took the important French Grand Prix, all with the 65-degree engine. Before the season ended tragedy was, once more, to strike Ferrari. On lap 2 of the Italian GP at Monza, Jim Clark (Lotus) and Von Trips collided while approaching the Parabolica. The Lotus spun harmlessly onto the grass, but the 156 F1 was catapulted up the grass bank. Von Trips was thrown out, and later died without having regained consciousness. Even more tragically, the car hurtled into the protective wire-mesh fencing killing 11 spectators.

Development work scheduled for the 1961-62 winter months was abruptly halted when Ferrari's chief engineer Carlo Chiti and team manager Tavoni walked out along with other senior staff. Needless to say there

Below: The 156 F1 was Ferrari's earliest mid-engine GP car. It was raced with 65-degree and 120-degree V-6s, and Phil Hill won the 1961 world drivers title with it.

was little progress toward the 1962 season, which would see Ferrari without a single major victory. Phil Hill was disgusted with the handling of the cars he had to drive; Enzo accused him of not trying. Hill left, too.

A new monocoque chassis was tested during the summer of 1963 to be mated with a proposed 1.5-liter 90-degree V-8. A redesigned V-6 engine with Bosch fuel injection was used for testing, the pump being located in the vee. In the hands of John Surtees, this car started the Italian Grand Prix from the pole, but suffered a bum piston after being in contention for 17 laps.

Once the new V-8 was ready, the new 158 F1 racer was hurriedly prepared for the Syracuse Grand Prix in April 1964. Though it was entered mainly as a trial, Surtees managed to bring it home 1st, average 102.63 mph. Bandini was 2nd in the V-6. In the next few events, however, the new V-8 racer failed to live up to its initial promise. Then, everything went right again at the German Grand Prix, and Surtees scored again, averaging 96.57 mph. A month later, he won the Italian GP, then placed 2nd in both the U.S. and Mexican GPs. The 1964 season turned out very well: Surtees won the world drivers crown on points, and Ferrari notched another manufacturers' title. Quite an achievement for a new design.

Also appearing at Monza that year was Ferrari's first flat 12 car, but it was only used in practice by Bandini. With a displacement of 1489cc (90.9 cid) it was designated the 1512 F1, and had a claimed 225 bhp. For the 1965 season both the 158 F1 and 1512 F1 were used, but neither managed a single outright win.

The 1.5-liter formula was replaced for the 1966 season by a dual-displacement one: 3000cc unblown or 1500cc supercharged. Franco Rocchi designed a new V-12 car with the idea that because of Ferrari's V-12 experience it made sense to revive that configuration. Tagged 312 F1, this car scored only two major

Above: Chris Amon does a bit of opposite-locking in an early version of the 312 Formula 1 car, probably at the British Grand Prix.

GP wins plus some minor placings between 1966 and 1969, so it could hardly be called a world-beater.

For 1970 there was a revival of the 12-cylinder boxer engine in the new 312 B. A prototype was tested before the 1969 Italian GP in the hope that it would be competitive, but further work was indicated. The first race appearance for the 312 B was in the hands of Jacky Ickx for the non-championship South African Grand Prix at Kyalami. It retired with falling oil pressure. It was not until the Austrian Grand Prix at the Osterreichring in August that the car showed its true abilities: Ickx won at 129.27 mph, Clay Regazzoni followed in 2nd, and Giunti took 7th. Next, Regazzoni captured the Italian GP. To finish off the season, Ickx won the Canadian and Mexican races, but had to be content with a 4th at Watkins Glen.

The 1971 campaign got off to a promising start as Mario Andretti won the Kyalami curtain-raiser. Wins also came at Brands Hatch, Ontario in California, and Hockenheim, all non-championship races. The only other major success was at Zandvoort in the Dutch Grand Prix, when the updated 312 B2 made its debut.

Late in 1974 Ferrari presented his new 312 T boxer, the T standing for *Transversale,* meaning transverse gearbox. Niki Lauda had joined the factory team, with Regazzoni continuing as number-two. For the first time in several years, Ferrari won the manufacturers title, and Lauda won the drivers championship.

Use of high air intakes behind the driver was banned beginning with the Spanish Grand Prix in 1976, so the 312 was redesigned to become the 312 T2. Lauda started strongly by winning the Brazilian, the South African, the Belgian, and Monaco events. But at the Nurburgring he had a horrible accident that would have caused most drivers to give up racing altogether. However, he came back, and in 1977 won the South African, German, and Dutch events. He also placed high enough in other points races to win his second drivers title, and gave Ferrari the manufacturers' crown for the third year in a row.

Despite these successes, the '77 season ended in acrimony when Lauda walked away from motor racing by refusing to run in the U.S. GP. Carlos Reutemann replaced him as team leader for 1978, with Gilles Villeneuve as his partner, but the magic was gone. Then, it came back in 1979 with the 312 T3 and T4 cars. Jody Scheckter was the driving champion, with Villeneuve runner-up. But Scheckter seemed

to lose his urge to win in 1980, and Villeneuve had to battle on without much success.

During the early part of 1980, Ferrari was reported to be working on a 1500cc twin-turbocharged V-6, which was formally unveiled in June. Cylinder banks were 120 degrees apart, leaving space for the turbochargers within the vee. It was obvious that this configuration would have heat dispersal problems, so there were lateral louvers in the engine cover and two additional radiators mounted in side pods. The 1496.4cc (91.3-cid) engine had very oversquare bore and stroke dimensions of 81 x 48.4mm (3.19 x 1.91 inches). With Lucas fuel injection and two KKK turbochargers, power output was at least 540 bhp. The 1981 season was an experimental year for this car, designated the 126 C. The main emphasis was on improving acceleration response (almost solved by the end of the season) and, of course, finding reliability.

One major problem remained: like many other Ferrari racing cars the 126C had atrocious handling, and something drastic had to be done. Ferrari called in Harvey Postlethwaite, a chassis and suspension expert from Britain. His work resulted in the 126 C2 for 1982. It had an entirely new chassis in which carbon fiber was used for the front and rear bulkheads and an aluminum

Above: A 312 B3 prototype from 1972 bears unusual nose treatment. Below: The late Gilles Villeneuve in the 126 C, shown rounding a curve at the 1981 Monaco GP.

honeycomb for the monocoque itself, the whole thing being glued together. Weight dropped below 590kg (1300 lbs), a saving of about 110 pounds over the earlier car. More power was extracted from the V-6, and claimed output was now 590 bhp, although this was probably a conservative figure. The revised suspension and a narrower transverse gearbox gave the handling needed to match such a powerful engine.

Once more, everything seemed to be coming together for Ferrari. It had a fast, reliable car and two exceptionally competent drivers,

Gilles Villeneuve and Didier Pironi. But, as it had before, tragedy struck again. While qualifying for the 1982 Belgian Grand Prix, Villeneuve was involved in one of the most horrifying accidents in racing history. His 126 C2 touched the rear wheels of a slower car, and was catapulted into the air. Villeneuve did not survive. Then, in a practice round for the German Grand Prix at Hockenheim, Pironi was following two other cars in heavy rain and was unable to see clearly. He touched the rear wheel of the car in front, and again the car somersaulted upwards. Fortunately, it landed right side up, but the car was completely wrecked. Pironi survived, but broke both thighs and an arm.

Now in his 85th year, Enzo Ferrari now has much less personal interest in grand prix racing than he did in his younger days. Yet such incidents must weigh heavily with him. But Ferrari is a single-minded man, and racing has always been the name of his game. For some two generations, the Ferrari marque and the history of automotive competition have been closely intertwined. And it's safe to say that this will continue to be true as long as there are Ferraris around to write new pages in the record books.

The Type 166 Mille Miglia barchetta

THE MOST SOUGHT-AFTER FERRARIS

Ferraris are not the only cult cars in the world, but today they are probably at the top of most enthusiasts' lists when it comes to desirability. Certainly few other marques have produced such a variety of different models that merit the kind of intense interest Ferraris enjoy.

In a sense, almost every Ferrari ever made is a collector's item. The possible exceptions are the mid-to late-'70s cars, which were more uniform in specification and produced in greater numbers than earlier types. Even so, it's tough to discount models like the

365 GT4BB and 512BB or the 308 GTB/GTS.

Why are Ferraris so coveted? Mainly because they seem to possess more of those qualities that make older cars desirable in the first place. These include low production (particularly true of early Ferrari models), unusual styling or engineering, exceptional craftsmanship, and stellar on-road performance. Most collectors would certainly agree that most Ferraris rate high in all these areas. But a Ferrari has a couple of extra things in its favor compared to other cars. For example, there's the mystique associ-

The Type 166 Mille Miglia berlinetta

The Type 340 Mexico berlinetta

The Type 375 Mille Miglia spyder

ated with the name, a legendary quality that's very much bound up with the marque's long racing history. There's also the unique dual-purpose aspect of many of Maranello's cars, an idea with great appeal among aficionados. Then, too, there's something about a Ferrari that transcends mere style and craftsmanship, something that elevates many models almost to the level of art. Even so, dyed-in-the-wool Ferrari lovers would be the first to tell you that these cars were not built to be put on a pedestal: they were — and still are — meant to be driven. Though a Ferrari may be very rare or very old, it is still best appreciated from behind the wheel.

Of course, not all Ferraris are equal in collector esteem, so it is possible to single out particularly noteworthy examples as the "best of the best." That's what we do here and in the following pages. Keep in mind that these particular cars are scarce and do not come up for sale very often. On the rare occasion when one does change hands, it will usually be a very swift

transaction involving a good deal of money.

So, here are the most collectible, the most desirable Ferraris — the uncommon, the exotic, the history-making models most of us can only dream about.

The 166 MM (Mille Miglia) was based on the early grand prix Ferrari, and had a 2.0-liter V-12 engine. It was built and raced in both berlinetta (closed coupe) and open barchetta ("little boat") form. Both types are desirable today, but it's the barchetta that still catches the eye. Small, elegant, well-proportioned, it remains one of the most fondly remembered Ferraris.

The 340 Mexico was powered by a 60-degree 4.1-liter V-12. It was designed to compete in the 1952 Carrera Panamericana, the famed Mexican Road Race. With this car and a victory, Enzo Ferrari hoped to crack the potentially lucrative U.S. market for high-performance European road cars. The Mexico's berlinetta body was shaped by Giovanni Michelotti and built by Vignale. The slab sides made it look more

227

The Type 212 Export barchetta

like a roadgoing GT than a racer built for dusty dirt trails, but the long wheelbase and powerful engine made this car ideally suited to the rigors of the romantic, long-distance Mexican event. It's still a stunning machine.

The 375 MM was a no-nonsense sports/racing coupe and more than a handful to drive, but no list of Ferrari's best would be complete without it. Its body was designed by Pinin Farina, and its 4.5-liter V-12 was engineered by Aurelio Lampredi. This was another Ferrari built primarily for long-distance com-

petition. Today, it has little competition as a car to stir the soul.

The 212 Export was similar in many ways to the 166 MM barchetta. Construction on both was carried out by Carrozzeria Touring, and both had the endearing roadster body style. The 212 model, however, had a longer wheelbase, minor differences around its grille, and lacked the MM's hood air scoop.

The 250 MM, introduced in 1953, was powered by a derivative of the Colombo short-block V-12 with a 3.0-liter displacement. Vignale created a very hand-

The Type 250 Mille Miglia berlinetta

The Type 375 Mille Miglia berlinetta

228

The Type 250 Testa Rossa

some spyder body for this chassis, and Pinin Farina designed a good-looking (though stubby) all-aluminum berlinetta with an unusual, almost round grille.

The 375 MM Spyder *was seen with a number of body variations. Some had headrests or tailfins faired into the bodywork, for example—rare but hardly exotic in the '50s. But the sleek, uncluttered Pinin Farina shape must surely be considered a milestone among open cars. It's one reason why this sports/racing machine remains in a class of one.*

The 250 Testa Rossa *is memorable not only for its laudable competition record but also for its appearance. The rare late-1957/early-1958 models with the pontoon fenders are some of the prettiest spyders ever devised. Unfortunately, the later "cutaway" style designed for better aerodynamics didn't live up to its promise. But as racers all the TRs did. With their 3.0-liter Colombo V-12, they took Ferrari to the World Sports Car Championship in 1958, 1960, and 1961.*
The 412 MI *was a one-of-a-kind item originally built for California Ferrari distributor John von*

The Type 250 GTO

The Type 250 Testa Rossa

The 250 GTO

The 250 GT Berlinetta Lusso

The 250 GT Berlinetta Lusso

Neumann in 1958. It carried the 4.1-liter four-cam V-12 from the 335 Sport installed in a 250 Testa Rossa chassis. This car was not very successful on the track, but it has won top concours honors in the years since. The letters MI stood for Monza/Indianapolis.
The 250 GTO is probably the one model every Ferrari fan would love to own. Trouble is, there were only 39 built, hardly enough to go around. This is certainly one of the handsomest race-and-ride sports cars ever to grace the automotive landscape. Today, the GTO could be described as an uncomfortable-riding car compared to newer Ferraris, but that's about the only drawback to driving one we can think of. From its

low-placed slotted nose to the uplifted tail, there's only one word appropriate for this superlative machine: thoroughbred.
The 250 GT berlinetta Lusso is neither rare nor expensive on the collector market, yet it is widely admired and avidly pursued. The reason is its styling: graceful, elegant, almost delicate, yet also dynamic in a way suggestive of its considerable performance. It was the first Ferrari road car equipped for really comfortable touring in the grand manner, offering the most tasteful, highest quality appointments seen from Maranello up to that time. Unfortunately, it was built for only two years. With all this, it's no wonder

The 275 GTB/4

The 250 LM

the Lusso became a classic in its own time.

The 250 LM (Le Mans) *was the first mid-engine Ferrari practical enough for the road, though it was clearly intended for competition. With its squat, muscular lines hinting only a little at sensuality, it could hardly be anything else. Most of those built had a 3.3-liter V-12 and should really be termed 275s, but Ferrari himself kept to the 250 designation in an effort to win homologation approval for this model as a GT-class racer. An impressive car then and now, on and off the track.*

The 275 GTB *was the replacement for the Lusso and, like it, was blessed with one of the truly great shapes of the '60s. It was the first Ferrari road car with all-independent suspension, but like many "consumer" Ferraris before and after it saw lots of action on race tracks all over the world. There was even a special competition version, the* 275 GTB/C, *a rare and desirable commodity today. Even more coveted are the nine open models built on the revised GTB/4 platform by Luigi Chinetti Jr.'s NART organization in the U.S. This series is simply another example of Pininfarina's mastery of line and form. It's a shape that still turns heads today, and probably will for as long as there are people who know and appreciate cars of uncompromising excellence.*

FERRARI SHOW CARS

Manufacturers and coachbuilders are at times prompted to let their fantasies run free with designs that not only delight but excite those who have an eye for the unusual. Such exercises usually are not meant to be practical and the products of the designers' fertile imaginations bear no relation to the functional. Some fantasies go sadly amiss and show a complete lack of knowledge of the automobile, resulting in a grotesque style.

Not all the Ferraris in this section were styled purely for show purposes and then set aside never to be seen again. Some were one-off creations for customers with aesthetic ideas of their own.

Apart from Pininfarina, whose relationship with Ferrari was and is unique, there were but one or two other designer/coachbuilders who produced either a one-off or show car.

Ferrari 375 America special coupe (1955): The coachwork was built on the normal chassis of the 375 AM and commissioned by Gianni Agnelli. Perhaps its most striking feature is the un-Ferrari-like treatment of the grille, which was squared and had a relatively fine mesh sloping in from the top of the radiator. The headlamps were at the extremities of the front fenders and the windshield was a wraparound type. The roof of the coupe was see-through perspex. Small tail fins extended from the rear of the driver/passenger compartment to the edge of the rear fender. A Pininfarina design and a striking one-off that would not be identified as a Ferrari.

Ferrari 250 GT special berlinetta (1963): Pininfarina designed and built this one-off for the London Motor Show. A series 250 chassis was used for the coachwork. While it is not a 250 GT berlinetta Lusso, in many respects it is very similar except for the nose treatment, which dipped. It also had window vents and the rear treatment was very clean. The styling at the front and rear appeared later on some 250 spyders.

Special Dino berlinetta (1965): The prototype coachwork of the Dino 206 was a most striking styling exercise. The nose had a full-width aperture treatment (the engine being mid-mounted) with four headlamps. In retrospect, the front styling was so unusual that it surely would have been a crowd-stopper. A Pininfarina design.

Ferrari 250 Le Mans road berlinetta (1965): The origin of this one-off model, prepared for the Geneva

The 365 P Berlinetta Speciale, 1966

Salon, was the 250 LM, although it would be difficult to imagine as the styling was very different. It had a stubbier hood, though the windshield rake was similar. Besides two doors in the normal positions, it had two other gullwing doors that were hinged fore and aft and opened when the normal doors were also open to allow easier entry and exit. The rear window was raked at a gradual angle over the rear engine deck, finishing with a slight upward spoiler which was a part of the body and not an afterthought. A low sleek car with plenty of charm, it was a Pininfarina design.

Racing Dino berlinetta *(1967):* An aerodynamic interpretation for the racing Dino, it featured a movable spoiler at the front end. The four headlights were deeply recessed. The hood was short with a low-raked wraparound windshield. The short roof was clear perspex and an integral part of the gullwing doors. The rear engine deck was of the sugar-scoop type and a fixed spoiler on two struts was attached to the rear deck. Alloy wheels were fitted. The model was never put into production and did not have any great aesthetic appeal. A Pininfarina design.

Ferrari 365P berlinetta *(1966-67):* Two of these models were built and at least one still exists. They were one-off models in each case, with a slight difference. For some unaccountable reason they had three seats side by side with the driver sitting in the center, which was hardly conducive to safe driving. It was engineered as a racing car, which doesn't really make

The 250 P/5 berlinetta, 1968

234

The P6 Berlinetta Speciale, 1968

much sense either. From front to rear the overall impression is one of a larger-scale 206 GT but with a clear perspex roof. The rear deck engine cover was of the sugar-scoop type. The wheels were the five-spoke alloy type. The second car was for Gianni Agnelli and he requested a large matte steel spoiler at the rear and an exposed fuel cap. A Pininfarina design, and a pretty car, but somewhat senseless.

Ferrari 250P special berlinetta *(1968)*: First shown at the Geneva Salon, this futuristic design showed a slight resemblance to the P series of sports/racing cars. It was never intended for racing and has probably never been driven, even though a 3.0-litre, 48-valve V-12 engine was installed amidships. It was only 38.6 inches high with fenders of swooping, elliptical form. Between the fenders and low down on the nose behind a full-width plastic cover were eight headlamps. At the rear an ostentatious venetian blind type group of louvers formed a wraparound tail which was high in relation to the remainder of the design. The windshield was very sharply raked and visibility was good all around. The air scoops for the mid-engine started near the front of the doors. The engine cover was clear perspex and the spare wheel was located at the rear of the longitudinally placed engine. Wheels were five-spoke alloy. In spite of its rather flamboyant styling it was pleasing to look at and purposeful in appearance. Apart from Geneva it was shown at Los Angeles, New York, and finally at Turin, when it was painted white. A similar body appeared on the Alfa Romeo 33 chassis.

A second P car, the P6, also for show and engineless, was produced, but without the ornamentation of the P5. It was more conventional in shape and the long low hood ended in a sharp nose with the normal four headlights behind clear perspex squares placed on either side of the nose. The back end was stumpy, without any real style and with transverse slats at the rear of the cockpit. Rear vision was minimal. It was a Pininfarina designed car and allegedly the Berlinetta Boxer was derived from the exercise.

Ferrari 512 S special berlinetta *(1969)*: Here Pininfarina demonstrated the logic of the wedge-shaped car taken to its extreme but with a style that few other designers could conceive. Shown at Turin in 1969, the body was formed on the rear-engined V-12 chassis of the 512 S. It was by no means as unconventional as the car Pininfarina was to show at Geneva in 1970.

The whole concept was aggressive-looking with long, slowly rising rear fenders, which started from just behind the front fenders. The low windshield was in line with the almost imperceptible slope of the hood, which had a sharp nose with a slit right across the front for the air intake. The windshield and doors were one piece that lifted at the front. The rear fenders and engine deck (with three rows of louvers) were one piece and the tail was semi-Kamm style. Headlamps were pop-up. The whole car was painted yellow and while rear vision was almost nonexistent, it was a design which could conceivably have made the circuits for sports racing.

Ferrari 512 Modulo *(1970)*: Dreamed up by Pininfarina, the Modulo was in all respects one of the wildest designs ever conceived and as such is considered either a work of superb architecture or a nightmare dreamed up by Pininfarina. It made its appearance at the Geneva Salon and created an enormous amount of interest. The coachwork was designed on a 512S chassis but obviously had no practical value.

With a clean flowing line running from the sharp low nose to the Kamm rear end, the whole is poetry in

The 512 S Berlinetta Speciale, 1969

motion, even if the car could only travel in a straight line due to the bodyline spats that covered the front wheels. It also had semi-spats over the rear wheels but these were, in fact, a part of the body and not removable. Both sets of spats had air inlets. The sharply raked windshield and the side windows form a complete unit that slides forward to allow entry and exit. Headlamps are recessed behind clear perspex covers. The interior is luxurious with padding covering the monocoque's sides and the instrument panel. Seats are body-hugging racing type. The original color of the coachwork was matte black with the appearance of a satin finish and a narrow red waistline around the car. The rear engine cover was bare metal with 24 holes for the air intakes that were fabricated from a transparent material. The maximum height was 44 inches.

Sigma Grand Prix *(1969):* Pininfarina presented this car at the 1969 Geneva Salon as his idea on the way Formula 1 racing cars should be built to ensure the safety of the driver. The concept was based on the 1968 Ferrari and incorporated a number of the V-12 components. Self-sealing fuel tanks and an automatic fire extinguishing system were among many features that were noted by motor racing authorities in Europe. Some of those have been incorporated in present day Formula 1 designs. The body styling, however, does not remotely follow that of today's cars where the driver sits right up front where his limbs are always in danger of being broken or crushed in a head-on collision with any immovable object.

Study CR 25 *(1974):* This somewhat large coupe was styled to achieve the best of almost everything from the effects of wind-tunnel tests. The object was to

The Modulo, 1970

solve scientifically the problems of aerodynamics relative to speed, comfort, safety, and fuel consumption. While some of this may have resulted from wind tunnel tests, the overall picture is not quite what Ferraris are about. However, it does have some pleasing aspects with relatively smooth lines and good all-round visibility. Its drag coefficient (wind resistance) is 0.25 (hence the designation CR25) and while this has been improved upon by other coupes, the figure is more than satisfactory. Two features in particular are notable—the use of a large front bumper that doubles as a spoiler and aerodynamic brakes on the body sides towards the rear of the cockpit.

There were, of course, other designers and coachbuilders who felt they had something to say where Ferraris were concerned, many of these were "one-offs" built to special customer requirements some of whom considered they could out-design the real artists. In the main, their efforts resulted in minor modifications.

Designers such as Fantuzzi, Neri and Bonacini, and Tom Meade were more than capable of translating Ferraris into road cars with a special appeal. On the other hand Drogo bodies are not particularly attractive, some are even outrageous.

The late '60s saw a decline in the specialist designer and builder, although a number of specialists have used various Ferrari chassis for their work. Felber, a Swiss stylist, produced the Felber FF, supposedly a replica, simulating the lines of the Spyder Corsa, but the effort was wasted as it represented nothing in particular. It was powered by the 330 GTC engine and used the GTC's suspension. Shown at Geneva in 1974 it was to be in limited production but it is doubtful whether there were any orders.

Giovanni Michelotti, who was a designer for Vignale during the 1950s, designed three bodies on Ferrari chassis during the '70s, none of which were of any particular merit. One was a spyder built for NART (North American Racing Team) with a front-mounted V-12 engine. Behind the driver/passenger seats was a targa roll bar, but the rear end upset the balance of the style. The radiator and headlamp treatment were reminders of some of the Exner styles on replicas. His next exercise, also for NART and exhibited at Geneva in 1975, was based on a 365 GTB/4 (Daytona) chassis and bore a striking likeness to the Corvette. Once more the radiator treatment was overly heavy. This car was entered by NART at Le Mans but was withdrawn, along with other NART cars when a dispute arose over the qualification of one of the entries.

The third Michelotti design for Felber was a doorless two-seat beach buggy with a front-mounted V-12. The sides were cut below the wheel-arch line. This car was shown at Geneva in 1976.

In 1975 Panther (England) built a special body on a 365 GTB/4 (Daytona) to the design of a customer, Gene Garfinkle. Apart from the restyling of the front end the main features behind the cockpit were two glass doors (gullwing style) and a deep rear window,

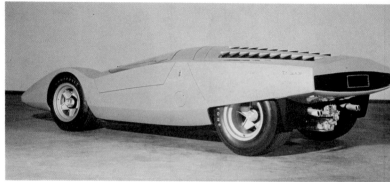

The 512 S Berlinetta Speciale, 1969

Drogo-bodied 250 GT

Drogo-bodied 250 GT

also glass. The whole appearance was that of a station wagon but it is difficult to see how passengers are supposed to enter the rear compartment other than having to scramble over the rear wheel arches! Borrani-type wire wheels replaced the usual five-spoke alloy type.

Fly Studio of Modena, a company run by Ing. Giacomo Caliri, who had worked for Ferrari on the body styling for the 312P and 512M sports racing cars built the cabriolet type body on the 365 GT4 2+2 chassis. It had a fixed center section between the windshield and the roof structure at the back. The roof had two upper panels that were removable, allowing a view of the open sky.

FERRARI'S AMERICAN DRIVERS

Phil Hill, Ritchie Ginther, and Pedro Rodriguez driving 156 F1s at the 1961 Italian Grand Prix

The first Ferrari seen in competition was the Type 125 Sport, driven by Franco Cortese at Piacenza in May 1947. Since then, there has been a bewildering array of grand prix, sports/racing, and gran turismo cars bearing the name Ferrari, and a great many drivers have made racing history with them. Some — notably Lorenzo Bandini, Alberto Ascari, and Wolfgang von Trips — were associated with the factory teams for years. Others were engaged for much shorter periods, as briefly as a single race in some instances. Thus, most of the great and near-great names in racing are inscribed on Ferrari's lengthy competition honor roll.

In the late '40s and early '50s, Enzo Ferrari had little trouble recruiting capable Italians to drive his cars. But even in the formative years of the Ferrari marque he was not reluctant to look beyond his homeland for the best talent he could find. Remember that, as with Scuderia Ferrari in the '30s, Enzo wanted to make racing pay. For him racing was not for fun, not a "gentleman's sport," but business. So, for example, when it came time to field a team for the races held in South America, he would ask prominent local pilots such as Juan Manuel Fangio and Froilan Gonzales to join his regular drivers on Team Ferrari. In all, only 21 Italians have driven for Ferrari in grands prix over the years, a fact that continues to infuriate the Italian press.

Naturally, Enzo was interested in seeking out the services of the best U.S. racers, which he did fairly early on. The first American to drive a GP Ferrari was Masten Gregory at the Buenos Aires event in January 1957. The race was run in two heats, and there were six Ferrari/Lancias entered. The track temperature was a torrid 140 degrees, oppressively hot for those drivers used to cooler climes. One was Englishman Peter Collins, who was one of the front runners when he handed over his car to Gregory, even though Gregory was not a member of the Ferrari team. Gregory then proceeded to win the second heat, giving the car a 3rd place overall. This was the only time Gregory drove in a grand prix for Ferrari, but he did drive sports/racing and gran turismo cars in many long-distance events for the factory.

The three most prominent Americans contracted for Formula 1 were Phil Hill, Richie Ginther, and Dan Gurney. Hill had been retained to drive sports/racing and GT Ferraris before he was given a seat in a grand prix car. That came for the German GP at the Nurburgring in August 1958. Hill was slated for the Formula 2 class behind the wheel of the V-6 156 F2 that Collins had taken to 2nd place in the Coupe de Vitesse race at Rheims. Hill was leading his class comfortably until he spun on a patch of oil, running off the course. The oil breather pipe that ran under the car was damaged, and he was forced to continue with oil spraying on the rear tires, which slowed him down considerably. In the end, he finished a creditable 5th in class and 9th overall. Hill ran two more races in 1958, the Italian Grand Prix at Monza and the Moroccan GP at Casablanca, taking 3rd place in both with the Dino 246 F1.

Masten Gregory, first American to drive a GP Ferrari

Phil Hill, first American to win the World Drivers' crown

239

Phil Hill in a Type 212 Export, which he once owned

Hill was a regular member of the factory team from then until the end of the 1962 season. During 1959 he ran the Dino 246 in eight GPs, scoring 2nd in the French and Italian events and 3rd in the German Grand Prix (run on the dangerous Avus track in two heats), with minor placings at Silverstone (Daily Express Trophy), Monaco, and Zandvoort. He crashed during the Portuguese Grand Prix, and retired at Sebring in the United States Grand Prix. A fairly satisfactory season all told.

By 1960 the Dino 246 had become outmoded. Although it took the first three places in that years' Italian GP, it did so mainly by default because most opponents stayed away, thinking their cars unsuitable for the banked Monza track. But the 246 did carry an American to a European GP win, the first since Jimmy Murphy and his Duesenberg captured the French Grand Prix in 1921. Hill had to work hard for this victory, but he won at an average speed of 132.07 mph and set a new lap record, 136.74 mph. He had only one retirement during the season (the French GP), and his second-highest placing was a 3rd at Monaco. But he could only manage low positions in the other five important contests.

The new 1.5-liter formula took effect for the 1961 grand prix schedule and, as usual, Ferrari was well ahead of the opposition with a new rear-engine car. At Monaco, Hill and Von Trips had 156 F1 cars with the 65-degree V-6 and Ginther the same model with a 120-degree V-6. Ferraris notched 2nd, 3rd, and 4th, with Hill taking 2nd place. For the remainder of the year, Hill drove the 120-degree V-6 car. The only time he was not among the top three finishers was at the French Grand Prix. Wins in the Belgian and Italian events gave him sufficient points to win the World

Drivers Championship, the first American ever to do so.

During the winter of 1961-62 work should have been progressing on improving an already good design for the 1962 season. However, there was a big blowup at Maranello that resulted in a walkout by chief engineer Carlo Chiti, team manager Tavoni, and a number of other senior staff. No one involved has ever said much about this episode, but it did cost Ferrari valuable time.

Throughout 1962, Hill complained about poor handling in the 156 F1. He was not the only team man to do so, but he was harder to ignore, and he had never really seen eye-to-eye with Enzo Ferrari. Hill was enigmatic as far as the Italians were concerned, and didn't hestitate in saying what was on his mind. Enzo, on the other hand, preferred to be aloof with his staff and perhaps even more so with his drivers. To Ferrari, the driver was an "accessory" to his creations, so it was little wonder that now and again drivers would feel neglected to the point of walking out. While Hill scored one 2nd and three 3rds in 1962, he was also a DNF on two occasions (one because of his digust at his car's handling). In the Italian Grand Prix, he placed a lowly 11th. Then, Ferrari accused Hill of not trying hard enough throughout the season, and they parted company after the Italian race.

Phil Hill was not only a fine grand prix driver but an expert sports/racing and GT competitor as well. He drove in many such races for Ferrari, and won his share of the team's many triumphs.

Ferrari also had Dan Gurney under contract for part of the 1959 season. His first race in the Dino 246 F1 was the French Grand Prix (also designated the European GP for 1959), but he was forced to retire

Dan Gurney, circa 1970

due to clutch trouble. His next GP was the German race. Dinos were sent for Tony Brooks, Hill, and Gurney, with a fourth car for Cliff Allison as backup. The race was run in two 30-lap heats. Each lasted one hour, and the placings were based on aggregate times. Brooks won the first heat, followed by Gurney and Hill. The second heat was something of a Ferrari processional, but the three drivers made a real race of it, crossing the finish line less than a second apart. Brooks won, with Gurney in 2nd.

Gurney ran in two more grands prix that season, finishing 3rd at the Portuguese race and 4th at Monza. After this, he did not drive for Ferrari again.

Richie Ginther had a two-year stint (1960-61) as a Ferrari team pilot. But it was not so much his competition skills as his ability as a test driver that made him such a good acquisition. Ginther was an engineer and a specialist in aircraft design. His contribution to the handling of Ferrari's race cars was the result of painstaking experimentation with spoilers front and rear, a significant advance in the art of race car design. Ferrari, of course, also took advantage of Ginther's driving skills in the sports/racing and gran turismo contests.

For the first championship event of the 1960 European season, the Monaco race, Ferrari produced his prototype rear-engine GP car that borrowed a number of components from the previous front-engine cars. It had a multi-tubular space frame mounting the Dino 246 engine coupled to a new five-speed transaxle. The drive passed from the engine through the gearbox to the clutch, mounted at the rear, then returned through the gearbox to the crown wheel and pinion. This car was put together hastily and, as a result, handled badly. Ginther, on his first drive as a member of the Ferrari team, could only place it 6th. The car was taken to Zandvoort for the Dutch Grand Prix, but it was a non-starter. Ginther's mount was a fron-engine Dino 246, but again he could only manage 6th.

During August, the 50-lap Silver City Trophy race was scheduled for the recently extended 2.65-mile Brands Hatch circuit in England. Ferrari sent over Dino 246s for Hill and Ginther, but they were outclassed by the lighter rear-engine British cars. Hill had to be content with 4th and Ginther 9th. At Monza, however, Ginther brought his car home in

Ritchie Ginther in the 156 F1 at the 1961 Rheims GP

Ritchie Ginther in the number 18 246 F1 (with Wolfgang von Trips) at the 1961 Italian Grand Prix

2nd. Before the season ended, he ran the Modena Grand Prix driving the 65-degree 156 F2. Again he was runner-up, with Von Trips in a similar car right behind.

The 1961 season was a little more satisfying for Ginther. Although he never crossed the line in 1st place, he managed a win at Monaco, two 3rds (Belgium and Britain), a 5th at Zandvoort, and an 8th in the German event.

Ferrari did not have much success during 1965 with its 1.5-liter 158 F1 V-8 and the very new 1512 engine (a 1.5-liter flat-12). For most of the season John Surtees and Lorenzo Bandini took turns driving the two cars without a victory. There was more bad luck: Surtees suffered a bad crash in a Lola T70 during the Canadian Can-Am time trials. His injuries kept him out of racing for quite a while, which

Mario Andretti, 1969

meant he had to miss the United States Grand Prix at Watkins Glen. To replace him, Bob Bondurant signed on and was given the 158 F1, but could only manage 9th place. It was Bondurant's only race as a Ferrari team driver.

During 1970, Ferrari won four of the 13 GPs counting towards the championship with the 3.0-liter flat-12 312 B. Over the winter months additional development work was completed, including many detail changes, to produce the 312/B2. It was ready in time for the first race of the 1971 season, at Kyalami in South Africa. Actually, there were no plans to race the new car, a good thing as Clay Regazzoni spun during practice and plowed into an earthen bank, tearing off the front of the car.

Three 312 Bs were fielded instead, driven by Jacky Ickx, Regazzoni, and a "new boy," Mario Andretti. Andretti clawed his way up to 2nd and, with four laps to go, was two seconds behind Denny Hulme in the new McLaren M19A. Then, the McLaren started weaving after losing a bolt from its right upper rear radius arm. Andretti shot by to score his first grand prix points. At the same time he raised the race speed record to 112.36 mph. His next two events were non-championship F1 races at Brands Hatch and Ontario Motor Speedway in California. Regazzoni won at Brands with the 312/B2, with Andretti 2nd. Andretti won the two-heat Questor Grand Prix at Ontario, leaving Ickx on the sideline after his collision with Siffert's BRM. The remainder of the '71 season was a letdown for Andretti. He failed to finish the Spanish and Dutch races, failed to qualify at Monaco, and could only manage a 4th at the Nurburgring and an unlucky 13th at Mosport Park in the Canadian Grand Prix. He also missed the Watkins Glen event to drive in a USAC race.

For 1972, Team Ferrari again ran with the 312/B2, but Andretti again had a lackluster year. In the five championship races he was a DNF at Buenos Aires and Jarama (Spain), took 4th at Kyalami, 6th at Watkins Glen, and 7th at Monza.

Throughout his varied racing career, Andretti has always been a top-class competitor in all types of cars, from Indy cars to grand prix machines to rapid stock cars to gutsy sprint cars. A very versatile and tenacious driver, Andretti has also piloted sports/racing and GT Ferraris under factory contract.

FERRARI MODEL DESIGNATIONS

The type or series designations given to various Ferrari models over the years has been a frequent source of confusion. In fact, it can still leave the uninitiated very bewildered. There are several reasons for this. First, there are at least three different model designation methods that have been used over the years, sometimes concurrently. Second, some Ferraris, particularly a few rare racing types, were given multiple designations by the factory depending on what purposes Il Commendatore had in mind. Third, chassis numbers do not correspond at all to models, body styles, or series, cars being numbered consecutively as they rolled out the door. And fourth, some letter designations like "C" mean different things depending on what model or year you're talking about. Despite the problems involved, however, let's try to sort all this out.

Apart from cars like the current Mondial 8, the designations of most Ferrari production models and racing types up to 1970 correspond to approximate cubic centimeter displacement of one cylinder (rounded off to the nearest whole number). For example, with the Type 125 multiply the type number by the number of cylinders — in this case 12 — and you find engine displacement roughly equivalent to 1500cc. This system is still in use, though it gives no clue to the number of cylinders. The current 400i has a V-12 with about 400cc per cylinder or a total displacement of 4800cc. The same system applies to the four-cylinder racing cars of the mid-'50s such as the 500 Mondial, but not all of them follow this practice as shown by the 750 Monza or 250 Testa Rossa, both of which had 3.0-liter engines.

When the six-cylinder cars were introduced a second system was devised keyed to engine size in liters and number of cylinders. Examples are the Dino 246 (2.4-liter V-6), the 308 series (3.0-liter V-8), and the 512 (5.0 liters, but a flat-12 configuration). This method was also applied to a few early inline six-cylinder cars such as the 118 LM, also known as the 376 LM (3.7-liter six), and the 121 LM or 446 S (4.4-liter six). The Superfast series is an exception to both methods. There, name was the chief identifier. However, the 400 Superamerica and 500 Superfast were true to the second system, being 4.0-liter and 5.0-liter models, respectively.

Ferrari chassis numbering is relatively straightforward after about 1949. Generally, even numbers in steps of two (0002, 0006, 0010, etc.) have been used

The Type 212 rolling chassis

for the competition cars (except for the single-seaters) while odd numbers two apart (0003, 0007, 0011, etc.) were reserved for road cars. At present, competition chassis numbers are below 1000. With the exception of the Dinos (including the 308 GT4), road car numbers are now over 31,000. The Dinos and 308 GT4 have their own five-figure series, even and two apart, with the numbers now into the 16,000s. There are also competition Dinos with three-figure chassis numbers, even and two apart, ending at 034. The 512M and 512S competition cars have four numbers, even figures starting at 1002 and ending at 1048.

It has never been Ferrari's practice to reserve a batch of chassis numbers for a particular model or series. If three or four models were available at the same time, they were numbered as they came out of the factory without regard for type. Thus, noting the highest and lowest chassis number of a particular model gives no indication of actual production, though the Dinos and 308 GT4 are again exceptions. Nor is it possible to separate, say, berlinettas from spyders within a series since the numbering also took no account of body style.

Ferrari serial number plates and many model designations also include prefix and/or suffix letters that give a clue to the purpose, body style, or even race history of that particular model. The following are the ones most commonly encountered:

A - Automatic transmission (as in 400 A)
AL - America series, long chassis
AM - America series (as in 340/342 America)
AT - America Tubolare

B - Berlinetta (Italian for "little sedan": a coupe)
BB - Berlinetta Boxer (as in 512 BBi)
C - Corsa (early sports cars), Competizione (early closed racing models), Coupe (as in 330 GTC)
CM - Carrera Mexico (Mexican Road Race)
E - Export (as in Type 212 Export)
ED/ET - Export Tubolare
EL - Export Lungo (long chassis)
EU - Europa (250 Europa lwb)
GT - Gran Turismo (grand touring car)
GTO - gran turismo omologato (literally, homologated grand touring)
I - Inter (as in Type 195/212 Inter series); also "Independent" (as on 250 TRI)
i - iniezione (fuel injection, as on 308 GTBi)
M - Modified (as on 512 M)
LM - Le Mans (as on 250 LM)
MM - Mille Miglia (as on Type 166 MM, 375 MM, etc.)
P - Prototipo (prototype, as on 330 P2)
S - Sport (as on Type 195 S); also Spyder (as on 275 GTS)
SA - Superamerica
SP - Sport Prototipo (sports prototype, as on 246 SP)
TR - Testa Rossa ("red head")

As noted throughout the text, certain Ferrari models have acquired nicknames that were not official factory nomenclature but which persist nonetheless, especially among enthusiasts. Examples are the 365 GTB/4 "Daytona," the 250 GT "Spyder California," and the 250 GT berlinetta "Lusso" (luxury).

The 250 Testa Rossa

SELECTED
SPECIFICATIONS

The latest in a long line of Ferrari V-12s: The 4.8-liter fuel-injected powerplant from the current 400 Automatic.

166 Inter
(coupe and cabriolet)

years	1948-50
number built	37

engine

configuration/placement	V-12 (60 degree)/front
bore, mm/in.	60/2.36
stroke, mm/in.	58.8/2.31
displacement, cc/ci	1995/121.5
valve operation	sohc
ignition	single distributor
spark plugs per cylinder	1
compression ratio	8.0:1
carburetion	1 Weber 32 DCF
bhp	110 at 6000 rpm

drivetrain

clutch	single dry plate
transmission	5 speed w/reverse, in unit with engine, non-synchromesh

chassis

wheelbase, mm/in.	2200/86.6
track, front, mm/in.	1270/50.0
track, rear, mm/in.	1250/49.2
suspension, front	independent; double wishbones, transverse leaf spring
suspension, rear	live axle; semi-elliptic leaf springs, trailing arms
brakes	hydraulic; aluminum drums, iron liners
wheels	Borrani wire; center lock, knockoff

performance (approx.)

top speed, mph	120
0-100 mph	27 seconds

---

212 Export (barchetta)

years	1950-53
number built	including the Inter model: 110

engine

configuration/placement	V-12 (60 degree)/front
bore, mm/in.	68/2.68
stroke, mm/in.	58.8/2.31
displacement, cc/ci	2562/156.3
valve operation	sohc
ignition	2 Marelli distributors
spark plugs per cylinder	1
compression ratio	8.0:1
carburetion	3 Weber 36 DCF
bhp	150 at 6500 rpm

drivetrain

clutch	single dry plate
transmission	5-speed w/reverse; non-synchromesh, in unit with engine

chassis

wheelbase, mm/in.	2250/88.6
track, front, mm/in.	1270/50.0
track, rear, mm/in.	1250/49.2
suspension, front	independent; double wishbones, transverse leaf spring
suspension, rear	live axle; semi-elliptic leaf springs, trailing arms
brakes	hydraulic; aluminum drums, iron liners
wheels	Borrani wire, center lock, knockoff

performance (approx.)

top speed, mph	140
0-100 mph	18.1 seconds

250 MM (Mille Miglia)

years	1952-53
number built	31

engine

configuration/placement	V-12 (60 degree)/front
bore, mm/in.	73/2.87
stroke, mm/in.	58.8/2.31
displacement, cc/ci	2953/180.2
valve operation	sohc
ignition	2 Marelli distributors
spark plugs per cylinder	1
compression ratio	9.0:1
carburetion	3 Weber 40 1F4C or 36DCF
bhp	240 at 7200

drivetrain

clutch	multiple disc
transmission	4-speed w/reverse; all synchromesh, in unit with engine

chassis

wheelbase, mm/in.	2400/94.5
track, front, mm/in.	1300/51.2
track, rear, mm/in.	1320/52.0
suspension, front	independent; double wishbones, transverse leaf spring
suspension, rear	live axle; semi-elliptic leaf springs, trailing arms
brakes	hydraulic; aluminum drums, iron liners
wheels	Borrani wire, center lock, knockoff

performance (approx.)

top speed, mph	158
0-100 mph	17 seconds

---

375 MM (Mille Miglia) (berlinetta & spyder)

years	1953-54
number built	not more than 18

engine

configuration/placement	V-12 (60 degree)/front
bore, mm/in.	80/3.20 (works cars) 84/3.36 (customer cars)
stroke, mm/in.	74.5/2.98 (works cars) 68/2.72 (customer cars)
displacement, cc/ci	4494/274.1 (works cars) 4522/275.8 (customer cars)
valve operation	sohc
ignition	2 Marelli magnetos
spark plugs per cylinder	1
compression ratio	9.0:1
carburetion	3 Weber 1F/4C or 42 DCZ
bhp	320 at 7000 rpm (works cars)
	340 at 7000 rpm (customer cars)

drivetrain

clutch	multiple disc
transmission	4-speed w/reverse, all synchromesh

chassis

wheelbase, mm/in.	2600/104.0
track, front, mm/in.	1325/53.0
track, rear, mm/in.	1320/52.8
suspension, front	independent; double wishbones, transverse leaf spring
suspension, rear	live axle, semi-elliptic leaf springs, trailing arms
brakes	hydraulic; aluminum drums, iron liners
wheels	Borrani wire; center lock, knockoff

performance (approx.)

top speed, mph	180 plus (depending on rear axle ratio)
0-100 mph	11.5 seconds

750 Monza
(spyder, sports/racing)

years	1954
number built	29

engine

configuration/placement	inline 4/front
bore, mm/in.	103/4.06
stroke, mm/in.	90/3.54
displacement, cc/ci	2999/183.0
valve operation	dohc
ignition	2 Marelli distributors
spark plugs per cylinder	2
compression ratio	8.6:1
carburetion	2 Weber 58 DCOA/3
bhp	260 at 6000 rpm

drivetrain

clutch	double dry plate
transmission	5-speed w/reverse; non-synchromesh, in unit with differential

chassis

wheelbase, mm/in.	2250/88.6
track, front, mm/in.	1278/50.3
track, rear, mm/in.	1284/50.6
suspension, front	independent; double wishbones, transverse leaf spring
suspension, rear	De Dion; transverse leaf springs, trailing arms
brakes	hydraulic; aluminum drums, iron liners
wheels	Borrani wire, center lock, knockoff

performance (approx.)

top speed, mph	164
0-100 mph	17 seconds

---

121 LM
(spyder, sports/racing)

years	1955
number built	4

engine

configuration/placement	inline 6/front
bore, mm/in.	102/4.02
stroke, mm/in.	90/3.54
displacement, cc/ci	4412/269.2
valve operation	dohc
ignition	coil
spark plugs per cylinder	2
compression ratio	8.6:1
carburetion	3 Weber 50 DCOA 3
bhp	330 at 6000 rpm

drivetrain

clutch	multiple disc
transmission	5-speed w/reverse; non-synchromesh, in unit with differential

chassis

wheelbase, mm/in.	2400/94.5
track, front, mm/in.	1278/50.3
track, rear, mm/in.	1284/50.6
suspension, front	independent; double wishbones, coil springs
suspension, rear	De Dion; transverse leaf springs, trailing arms
brakes	hydraulic; aluminum drums, iron liners
wheels	Borrani wire, center lock, knockoff

performance (approx.)

top speed, mph	170
0-100 mph	16 seconds

250 Testa Rossa
(spyder)

years	1958-61
number built	33

engine

configuration/placement	V-12 (60 degree)/front
bore, mm/in.	73/2.87
stroke, mm/in.	58.8/2.31
displacement, cc/ci	2953/180.2
valve operation	sohc
ignition	2 Marelli distributors
spark plugs per cylinder	1
compression ratio	9.8:1
carburetion	6 Weber 38 DCN
bhp	300 at 7200 rpm

drivetrain

clutch	single dry plate
transmission	4-speed; all synchromesh, in unit with engine

chassis

wheelbase, mm/in.	2350/92.5
track, front, mm/in.	1308/51.5
track, rear, mm/in.	1300/51.2
suspension, front	independent; double wishbones, coil springs
suspension, rear	live axle; semi-elliptic leaf springs, trailing arms
brakes	hydraulic; aluminum drums, iron liners
wheels	Borrani wire, center lock, knockoff

performance (approx.)

top speed, mph	167
0-100 mph	16 seconds

---

250 GT
(short-wheelbase berlinetta)

years	1959-62
number built	175

engine

configuration/placement	V-12 (60 degree)/front
bore, mm/in.	73/2.87
stroke, mm/in.	58.8/2.31
displacement, cc/ci	2953/180.2
valve operation	sohc
ignition	2 Marelli distributors
spark plugs per cylinder	1
compression ratio	9.2:1
carburetion	3 Weber 40 DCL6 or 3 Weber 36 DCL3 (road cars)
	3 Weber 40 DCL6 or 3 Weber 46 DCL3 or 3 Weber 46 DCF3 (competition)
bhp	280 at 7000 rpm (competition)
	240 at 7000 rpm (road car)

drivetrain

clutch	single dry plate
transmission	4 speed w/reverse in unit with engine, all synchromesh

chassis

wheelbase, mm/in.	2400/94.5
track, front, mm/in.	1354/53.3
track, rear, mm/in.	1349/53.1
suspension, front	independent; double wishbones, coil springs
suspension, rear	live axle; semi-elliptic leaf springs, trailing arms
brakes	disc
wheels	Borrani wire, center lock, knockoff

performance (approx.)

top speed, mph	156
0-100 mph	23 seconds

400 Superamerica (coupe)

years	1961-64
number built	45

engine

configuration/placement	V-12 (60 degree)/front
bore, mm/in.	77/3.03
stroke, mm/in.	71/2.80
displacement, cc/ci	3967/242.1
valve operation	sohc
ignition	coil
spark plugs per cylinder	1
compression ratio	8.8:1
carburetion	3 Weber 46 DCF
bhp	340 at 7000 rpm

drivetrain

clutch	single dry plate
transmission	4-speed w/reverse, all synchromesh

chassis

wheelbase, mm/in.	2420, 2600/95.3, 102.4
track, front, mm/in.	1359, 1395/53.5, 54.9
track, rear, mm/in.	1350, 1387/53.1, 54.6
suspension, front	independent; double wishbones, coil springs
suspension, rear	live axle; semi-elliptic leaf springs, trailing arms
brakes	disc
wheels	Borrani wire; center lock, knockoff

performance (approx.)

top speed, mph	160
0-100 mph	18 seconds

---

250 GTO (berlinetta)

years	1962-64
number built	39

engine

configuration/placement	V-12 (60 degree)/front
bore, mm/in.	73/2.87
stroke, mm/in.	58.8
displacement, cc/ci	2953/180.2
valve operation	sohc
ignition	single distributor
spark plugs per cylinder	1
compression ratio	9.8:1
carburetion	6 Weber 36 DCN
bhp	280 at 7500 rpm

drivetrain

clutch	single dry plate
transmission	5-speed w/reverse; synchromesh, in unit with engine

chassis

wheelbase, mm/in.	2600/102.4
track, front, mm/in.	1354/53.3
track, rear, mm/in.	1349/53.1
suspension, front	independent; double wishbones, coil springs
suspension, rear	live axle; semi-elliptic leaf springs, trailing arms
brakes	disc
wheels	Borrani wire; center lock, knockoff

performance (approx.)

top speed, mph	176
0-100 mph	14.1 seconds

250 LM (berlinetta)

years	1963-66
number built	35

engine

configuration/placement	V-12 (60 degree)/mid
bore, mm/in.	77/3.03
stroke, mm/in.	58.8/2.31
displacement, cc/ci	3286/200.5
valve operation	sohc
ignition	coil
spark plugs per cylinder	1
compression ratio	9.8:1
carburetion	6 Weber 38 DCN
bhp	305 at 7500 rpm

drivetrain

clutch	single dry plate
transmission	5-speed w/reverse; non-synchromesh, in unit with differential

chassis

wheelbase, mm/in.	2400/94.5
track, front, mm/in.	1350/53.1
track, rear, mm/in.	1340/52.7
suspension, front	independent; double wishbones, coil springs
suspension, rear	as for front
brakes	disc
wheels	Borrani wire; center lock, knockoff

performance (approx.)

top speed, mph	160
0-100 mph	12 seconds

---

330 GT 2 + 2 (coupe)

years	1965-66
number built	455

engine

configuration/placement	V-12 (60 degree)/front
bore, mm/in.	77/3.03
stroke, mm/in.	71/2.80
displacement, cc/ci	3967/242.1
valve operation	sohc
ignition	coil
spark plugs per cylinder	1
compression ratio	8.8:1
carburetion	3 Weber 40 DCZ 6
bhp	300 at 6600 rpm

drivetrain

clutch	single dry plate
transmission	5-speed w/reverse; all synchromesh, rear mounted

chassis

wheelbase, mm/in.	2650/104.3
track, front, mm/in.	1397/55.0
track, rear, mm/in.	1389/54.7
suspension, front	independent; double wishbones, coil springs
suspension, rear	live axle, semi-elliptic leaf springs, trailing arms
brakes	disc
wheels	Borrani wire, center lock, knockoff

performance (approx.)

top speed, mph	150
0-100 mph	17 seconds

275 GTB/4 (berlinetta)

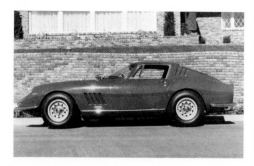

years	1966-68
number built	350

engine

configuration/placement	V-12 (60 degree)/front
bore, mm/in.	77/3.03
stroke, mm/in.	58.8/2.31
displacement, cc/ci	3286/200.5
valve operation	dohc
ignition	coil
spark plugs per cylinder	1
compression ratio	9.2:1
carburetion	6 Weber 40 DCN 17
bhp	300 at 8000 rpm

drivetrain

clutch	single dry plate
transmission	5-speed w/reverse; all synchromesh, in unit with differential

chassis

wheelbase, mm/in.	2400/94.5
track, front, mm/in.	1401/55.2
track, rear, mm/in.	1417/55.8
suspension, front	independent; double wishbones, coil springs
suspension, rear	as for front
brakes	disc
wheels	Campagnolo light alloy

performance (approx.)

top speed, mph	155
0-100 mph	15 seconds

365 GTB/4 (Daytona) (berlinetta & spyder)

years	1968-73
number built	1300

engine

configuration/placement	V-12 (60 degree)/front
bore, mm/in.	81/3.19
stroke, mm/in.	71/2.80
displacement, cc/ci	4390/267.9
valve operation	dohc
ignition	twin distributor
spark plugs per cylinder	1
compression ratio	8.8:1
carburetion	6 Weber 40 DCN 20
bhp	352 at 7500 rpm

drivetrain

clutch	single dry plate
transmission	5-speed w/reverse, in unit with differential

chassis

wheelbase, mm/in.	2400/94.5
track, front, mm/in.	1440/56.7
track, rear, mm/in.	1425/56.1
suspension, front	independent; double wishbones, coil springs
suspension, rear	as for front
brakes	disc
wheels	Cromodora 5-spoke light alloy

performance (approx.)

top speed, mph	174
0-100 mph	18.3 seconds

Dino 246 GT/GTS
(berlinetta & spyder)

years	1969-74 (Dino 246 GT), 1972-74 (Dino 246 GTS)
number built	4000 plus

engine

configuration/placement	V-6 (65 degree)/transverse mid-engine
bore, mm/in.	92.5/3.64
stroke, mm/in.	60/2.36
displacement, cc/ci	2418/147.6
valve operation	dohc
ignition	coil
spark plugs per cylinder	1
compression ratio	9.0:1
carburetion	3 Weber 40 DCN F/7
bhp	195 at 7600 rpm

drivetrain

clutch	single dry plate
transmission	5-speed w/reverse; all synchromesh, in unit with differential

chassis

wheelbase, mm/in.	2336/92.0
track, front, mm/in.	1427/56.2
track, rear, mm/in.	1430/56.3
suspension, front	independent; double wishbones, coil springs, anti-roll bar
suspension, rear	as for front
brakes	disc
wheels	Cromodora light alloy

performance (approx.)

top speed, mph	146
0-100 mph	9 seconds

365 GTC/4 (coupe)

years	1971-72
number built	500

engine

configuration/placement	V-12 (60 degree)/front
bore, mm/in.	81/3.19
stroke, mm/in.	71/2.80
displacement, cc/ci	4390/267.9
valve operation	dohc
ignition	single distributor
spark plugs per cylinder	1
compression ratio	8.8:1
carburetion	6 Weber DCOE sidedraft
bhp	320 at 6200 rpm

drivetrain

clutch	single dry plate
transmission	5-speed w/reverse, all synchromesh, in unit with engine

chassis

wheelbase, mm/in.	2500/98.4
track, front, mm/in.	1470/57.9
track, rear, mm/in.	1470/57.9
suspension, front	independent; double wishbones, coil springs
suspension, rear	as for front but with hydropneumatic self-leveling
brakes	disc
wheels	Cromodora light alloy

performance (approx.)

top speed, mph	150
0-100 mph	14 seconds

308 GTBi/GTSi
(berlinetta & spyder)

years	1975 - date
number built	not available

engine
configuration/placement	V-8 (90 degree)/transverse mid-engine
bore, mm/in.	81/3.19
stroke, mm/in.	71/2.80
displacement, cc/ci	2927/178.6
valve operation	dohc
ignition	coil
spark plugs per cylinder	1
compression ratio	8.8:1
carburetion	4 Weber 40 DCNF (original); now Bosch fuel injection
bhp	quoted from 205 to 240 at 6600 rpm

drivetrain
clutch	single dry plate
transmission	5-speed w/reverse; all synchromesh, in unit with engine

chassis
wheelbase, mm/in.	2340/92.1
track, front, mm/in.	1460/57.5
track, rear, mm/in.	1460/57.5
suspension, front	independent; double wishbones, coil springs
suspension, rear	as for front
brakes	disc
wheels	Cromadora light alloy

performance (approx.)
top speed, mph	150
0-100 mph	11 seconds

---

512 BBi (berlinetta)

years	1976 - date
number built	not available

engine
configuration/placement	flat 12/rear
bore, mm/in.	82/3.23
stroke, mm/in.	78/3.07
displacement, cc/ci	4942/301.6
valve operation	dohc
ignition	1 distributor and electronic ignition
spark plugs per cylinder	1
compression ratio	9.2:1
carburetion	originally 4 Weber 40 LF/3C; now Bosch fuel injection
bhp	360 at 6200 rpm

drivetrain
clutch	multiple disc
transmission	5-speed w/reverse; all synchromesh, in unit with engine

chassis
wheelbase, mm/in.	2500/98.4
track, front, mm/in.	1500/59.1
track, rear, mm/in.	1563/61.5
suspension, front	independent; double wishbones, coil springs
suspension, rear	as for front
brakes	disc
wheels	Cromadora light alloy

performance (approx.)
top speed, mph	188
0-100 mph	10 seconds

400i Automatic

years	1979 - date
number built	not available

engine

configuration/placement	V-12 (60 degree)/front
bore, mm/in.	81/3.19
stroke, mm/in.	77/3.03
displacement, cc/ci	4823/294.3
valve operation	dohc
ignition	single Marelli distributor
spark plugs per cylinder	1
compression ratio	8.8:1
carburetion	Bosch fuel injection
bhp	310 at 6400 rpm

drivetrain

clutch	not applicable
transmission	GM Turbo-Hydramatic; torque converter w/3-speed planetary gearbox

chassis

wheelbase, mm/in.	2700/106.3
track, front, mm/in.	1470/57.9
track, rear, mm/in.	1500/59.1
suspension, front	independent; double wishbones, coil springs
suspension, rear	as for front with hydropneumatic self leveling
brakes	discs
wheels	Cromadora light alloy

performance (approx.)

top speed, mph	145
0-100 mph	21 seconds

Mondial 8
(berlinetta 2 + 2)

years	1980 - date
number built	not available

engine

configuration/placement	V-8 (90 degree) transverse mid-engine
bore, mm/in.	81/3.18
stroke, mm/in.	71/2.80
displacement, cc/ci	2927/178.6
valve operation	dohc
ignition	coil
spark plugs per cylinder	1
compression ratio	8.8:1
carburetion	Bosch fuel injection
bhp	214 at 7500 rpm

drivetrain

clutch	single dry plate
transmission	5-speed w/reverse; all synchromesh, in unit with engine

chassis

wheelbase, mm/in.	2650/104.3
track, front, mm/in.	1495/58.9
track, rear, mm/in.	1517/59.8
suspension, front	independent; double wishbones, coil springs
suspension, rear	as for front
brakes	disc
wheels	Cromadora light alloy

performance (approx.)

top speed, mph	145
0-100 mph	12 seconds